ABUELO

A "MEMOIR"

RYAN DIAZ

Copyright © 2024 by Ryan Díaz.

All rights reserved.

No part of this publication may be reproduced, distributed, or transmitted in any form or by any means, including photocopying, recording, or other electronic or mechanical methods, without the prior written permission of the publisher, except as permitted by U.S. copyright law. For permission requests, contact Alternative Book Press.

The story, all names, characters, and incidents portrayed in this production are fictitious. No identification with actual persons (living or deceased), places, buildings, and products is intended or should be inferred.

Cover design by A Vague Idea.

Introduction:

On Memory and "Memoirs"

No one sets out to write a memoir because they believe their lives are particularly interesting. Most often, they're not, and those that are, are that rare breed of individual whose lives are prepackaged for literary greatness. The rest of us are trying to make sense of our very ordinary stories. We've tried it all—therapy, religion, alcohol, you name it, and when those failed, we turned to literature. We're those foolish individuals who believe that writing things down helps heal those wounded parts of us we've buried under our vices of choice. I can't say it works, but bookstores are still filled with our failed efforts at self-exorcism.

When I began this project, I thought writing a memoir would be simple. Retelling one's life story is undoubtedly easier than conjuring up a fictional world with fictional characters and fictional emotions (though one could argue that all fiction's fueled by reality, that is, the author's reality, the inner life that seeps through the subconscious and into the characters we create).

At least, that's what I thought.

Unlike fiction, a memoir relies on one's memory, the events we store in the neocortex, in hopes of transferring them to paper. But memory's a tricky thing. How do we know if our memories are real? Do things really happen as we remember them, or are our memories simply projections, useful fictions we construct to make sense of the world around us, abstractions we build with actual events?

I have this memory of my grandfather so vivid that I can't help but believe it's real. We're sitting on his porch in Puerto Rico, staring out onto the water-soaked street, sheets of summer rain beating against the pavement like a drumline, lightning streaking through the sky; a purple blur of electric fire. As if appearing out of the ether—a horse and a rider shrouded in shadow and rain. The horse and the rider stare back at me. His almond skin is slick with moisture, and, in the darkness, he merges into his horse like a centaur; two creatures becoming one.

I still taste the air on my tongue as the cooling sensation of rain slowly robs my skin of the island's oppressive heat. I still hear my grandfather's heart beating in his chest as I curl up in his arms, the steady thump of his heart rattling against his ribs like a conga player drumming out a beat. It's all there, at the forefront of my mind, as vivid as the computer before me and the clack of the keys as I type these words. But there's something else, a vague impression that none of it is authentic, that my memory of the horse and rider is nothing but an amalgamation of memories, useful scraps pieced together by my subconscious for reasons beyond my conscious mind. Herein lies my issue. How can I write a memoir if I can't tell the difference between what's true and what's fiction?

The book you're about to read is a novelization of real events, a faux memoir, if you will. I say that in case the fact-checkers come for me, though the one expert on my life qualified enough to critique this work is also the author and, as stated above, I've arrived at the limits of my own self-knowledge. While most things happened as stated, some events and people have merged into an amalgam of memory and self-interest (no one really remembers things as they were, anyways).

In this, I find kinship with those gospel writers who wrote a detailed account about a carpenter from Nazareth while playing fast and loose with dates and times and apparently without losing a grain of truth.

I can't speak for the characterization of the friends and family who might appear in the book. They, too, are victims of the fickle way memories encode people into our brains. We never truly see people for who they are. We see them as reflections of light bouncing back over and through our corneas, interpreted and reinterpreted by firing neurons until our brain registers another life outside our own. In the end, we're left with a portrait, an artist's rendering, and no matter how life-like the portrait, we're ultimately left with the illusion of life. Every person we've met and will ever meet exists only as we understand them, the real them, trapped between the plates of their skulls, known only to God and their ten-dollar shrink.

This begs the question, why should you bother reading this book? Surely, you'd be better off reading something real? Like one of those celebrity memoirs—those deep and insightful looks into the lives of the rich and famous, written in their own hand and certainly not by an underpaid ghostwriter lost in the halls of Penguin or HarperCollins.

Although, this course of action assumes that something must be real to be true, and that, dear reader, is often never the case.

Reality belongs to the realm of physics. Physics tells us how and when, what and who, but truth tells us why, and the great question "why" belongs to theology, philosophy, poetry, and art. Truth can't be reduced to what we can observe, it's far larger than that, and while this book plays with reality, I'd like to believe that it's true.

So, yes, cards on the table, I failed to write a memoir. But I like to think that in failing to recall things as they were, I get the opportunity to depict things as they are, that is, the truth. I'll reserve my judgment as to whether this book says anything true. Ultimately that job falls to you, the reader.

We're all, in the end, unreliable narrators, writing fiction with our lives in hopes of finding meaning. Writers are the ones foolish enough to write it down and put it into print. Posterity will decide whether this author's truth is worthy of discussion, and if not, I ask that you pass the copy along to someone else. Maybe they'll find this jumbled mess of memories useful.

Who knows, maybe you will too.

Chapter 1:

The Flight

I woke up with a start. The cabin was still dark. The movie I was watching on the tiny LCD in front of me was over, the credits scrolling down the black screen like rain sliding down a window. I grabbed my water bottle and swished the water 'round before taking a sip. My ears popped. The plane descended.

A few minutes later, the pilot got on the intercom to announce that we were making our descent. The cabin lights turned on and the flight attendants made their way down the aisle with black garbage bags. One flight attendant, a young man with blond hair, pointed at my water bottle.

"Are you finished with that?" He asked.

His teeth were shockingly white, like little marble tombstones arranged in neat rows on a red hill. I closed my mouth, all too aware of my yellowing teeth, victims of poor dental hygiene and too many cups of coffee. I handed him the empty bottle, but before I could thank him, he was already on to the next row, to blind another set of passengers with his impossible rows of pearly whites.

I looked over at my wife. She was still asleep, slumped against the window with only a neck pillow propping up her head. I hated those things. She once got me one as a gift. It was gray, and according to her research, it was highly recommended. I used it five minutes into our honeymoon before stowing it under my seat. It felt like I was suffocating. It was like wearing a noose, and I became convinced that it only worked because the pillow cut off circulation to the brain, like a prize MMA fighter choking out his opponent with a well-placed rear naked choke. When I told my wife that, she laughed and took the pillow for herself, and something inside me told me that might have been her plan all along.

That was five years ago; when we were young and dumb and still believed that love was enough.

The pilot got on the intercom again. We were twenty minutes out.

I put my tray table up and lifted my seat. I started to feel nervous. I took a deep breath and closed my eyes. It wasn't landing that bothered me. You fly enough and you forget all about the dangers involved, acting as if it was completely normal to fly a metal comet through the sky. It wasn't the flying that bothered me, either. I was more nervous about where we were going. It had been ten years since I last flew to Puerto Rico. Back then, I swore I'd never come back, let alone with my wife and my in-laws on vacation.

You see, that island and I have a complicated history. It started when I was young, unsure of myself and my identity, disconnected from my family's ancestral home, and always the tourist looking to belong.

The plane rumbled.

The flight attendants gave each other a knowing look and dashed to the end of the cabin to their seats. My wife woke up as the captain announced that we were experiencing a bit of turbulence. Her tired eyes opened in fear. She gripped my arm and pulled away from the window.

The plane rattled again, this time enough to move us in our seats. I peered outside the open window. The sky was black, and in the distance, thunder flashed. A storm lay between us and the safety of a landing strip. The plane convulsed and someone up in first-class screamed. My wife clamped her hand around my arm, the plane kept rumbling, and in the row in front of us, someone prayed.

"Dios te salve, María. Llena eres de gracia: El Señor es contigo. Bendita tú eres entre todas las mujeres. Y bendito es el fruto de tu vientre: Jesús. Santa María, Madre de Dios, ruega por nosotros pecadores, ahora y en la hora de nuestra muerte."

Her words rose and fell with the rumblings of the plane, rising as the plane shuddered, falling when we hit a bit of calm.

Despite my lackluster Spanish, I recognized the Hail Mary, and even though I wasn't Catholic, I appreciated the idea that prayer wasn't totally dependent on us, and that when worse comes to worst, we could rely on the prayers of others. A reminder that, despite our loneliness, we were never truly alone.

The plane lurched, this time sending us forward in our seats. The seatbelt pressed against my stomach, cutting into my skin as it worked to hold me in place.

The words came faster now, the words of the Hail Mary blending and transcending language, a true prayer of the heart, a groaning no one knew but God.

But I wasn't afraid. Rough air was a part of flying. We were perfectly safe. All the signs were there. There were no oxygen masks to be seen, and the attendants casually chatted behind us, the blond one trying to talk up his coworker, flashing his smile in hopes that it seduced as much as it stunned. Once we were out of the storm, all we had to do was land, deplane, and go about our lives as if nothing ever happened.

But when a plane shakes and the air gets bumpy, it's easy to see why we imagine the worst. Everything's out of our power, we're at the mercy of the weather and the pilot's skill, hoping that the latter wins out over the former. Up in the sky, we feel truly vulnerable, and a primal fear takes over. In an age where it's easy for certain classes of people to feel safe, we grow used to life's certainty and forget that certainty's a veneer, a clever lie we like to call normalcy, forgetting that all living's predicated on risk.

We live most of our lives balancing on a knife's edge, ignorant of the pitfalls, and that forces beyond our control lie in wait, ready to tip scales. We never notice, that's the point of civilization. We got rid of those fears when we learned to gather in groups and build walls. Now, our fears are existential. We fear for our meaning and our place in the world. These are privileged fears, fears that are afforded to the middle class and the moderately wealthy.

But every so often, those primal fears emerge, and we're left to face our true enemy, death. The one we're all trying to escape, pretending that creams and diets will keep him at bay. Putting off death does more harm than good. You see, it's in facing death that we learn how to live. That's life's great irony, that the one thing we fear is the only thing capable of teaching us how to live fearlessly.

As our plane trembled and quivered, and my wife dug her head into my chest, I thought about my life, the years I've lived, and how a tiny island in the middle of the Caribbean became the sight of my becoming. Yet, paradoxically, the place of my greatest regret.

Those are the things you try not to remember. The little inklings we keep tucked away in the back of our minds behind the cobwebs, and old Christmas decorations, shuttered up and sheltered from the conscience. Collecting dust in hopes that, one day, our memories fail us, and our regrets will be left to rot somewhere in the past.

I had no such luxury.

I felt my ears pop, we descended, and all those memories flooded back. I closed my eyes and swallowed hard. My ears popped again, everything was clearer, the rumbling of the plane, the worried voices, and the steady clack of the rain against the wings. I saw them in the back of my eyelids, old faces, growing clearer and clearer as the plane dipped its nose and committed to its descent. Like in the movies, it all came at once, a flood of memory like water from a dam, drowning my prefrontal cortex in names and places and people, rising from the muck of my subconscious. Among them, my grandfather, as I saw him as a boy, strong, and wise. Gray, hunched over his garden raking dirt and planting seeds, calling me to join him, offering me his watering can.

The cabin lights turned back on, the attendants were up, and the plane was still. I looked out the window and we were past the cloud cover. I saw the sea, dark and ominous, a giant blue maw, hungry and waiting. Beyond it, a little green emerald, Puerto Rico.

My wife sat up. The fear was gone. She turned her head and watched as the emerald grew into a mountain, its smooth surface growing hills and towns as if we witnessed some spontaneous act of creation. There I was, half-watching, half lost in memory, waiting for the familiar thump, and the sound of clapping hands.

Chapter 2:

1998

It was the first time I remember flying.

My mother and I were in a cab headed to JFK. My father was still at work and had promised to meet us a few weeks after his meetings were done. It was a red-eye, and being about six years of age at the time, I spent the trip to the airport in and out of sleep. I fought desperately to keep my eyes open, but every few minutes or so, my eyelids shut on their own accord and the cab's interior faded into a sea of black.

In those stolen minutes, time moved differently. Progress became meaningless. You felt weightless and weighed down all at once, drifting somewhere between the infinite expanse of space and the crushing weight of the deep. There I was, somewhere in the middle, a young boy, unable to tell the difference between being asleep and being awake.

The road was quiet, and the smell of the taxicab was suffocating. My mother cracked the window and leaned with her head in the breeze like a whale breaching the surface of the sea. I didn't mind, or maybe I didn't notice, my brain muddled by exhaustion, too tired to notice the smell—a toxic combination of stale air freshener, cigarette smoke, and the putrid stench of body odor. But we wouldn't have to suffer for much longer.

The dim glow of yellow streetlights darted overhead as we zipped down the Grand Central, cutting through the heart of a sleeping Queens. The ride took no time at all, maybe twenty minutes tops, but then again, I was still learning to tell time. At that age, time was infinite. Five minutes could feel like an eon and an hour an eternity.

You can never trust a child's sense of time. They haven't lived long enough to know its value, and they don't know how to mark its passing. The minute and hour hands might as well be decorations, to the child, they're meaningless.

Children measure life in moments, and when time itself seems infinite, why bother learning to keep track? Sure, I could've told you the time, but those numbers were an abstraction, an answer given to satisfy pestering adults. Eight AM and Eight PM might as well have been the same, the twelve hours between them were timeless.

The cab pulled off the highway and into the airport. My mother paid the taxi and muttered something about inflation before handing the man his money, another meaningless concept for a six-year-old who only knew the difference between nickels and dimes.

My mom pulled me by the hand and dragged the luggage behind her. I woke up. Unlike the warm, dark confines of the cab, the airport was bright and cold and smelled of that impersonal disinfectant that permeates public spaces. I didn't say much. My mom was focused. She had this look, and all conversation ceased when she put it on. Even my father knew the look. She wrinkled her brow and pursed her lips, her eyes locked on some invisible target in the distance. My mother always seemed two seconds away from dissolving into a frantic frenzy. I learned later that this was anxiety. She hated traveling, at least traveling alone, and it didn't take much to send her into a tailspin.

I distinctly remember getting lost on our way home from school. You would think that she'd have the route down. I attended the same school all my life and the drive was always the same. At twelve, you could've put me behind the wheel, and barring an accident, I knew the fastest way to get us home. But my mom hated traveling, she hated driving. Maybe she hated the responsibility of being in charge. Perhaps she was too used to my father taking the wheel.

But luckily for us, we made it to our gate without any diversions, and we even had time to peruse the useless shops that dotted the terminal. My mom got us bagels before picking up a coffee, and a magazine, *US* or *People,* one of those tabloids specially designed to kill time between connecting flights.

They called our names. We rushed from the shops to the gate and made it in time for my mother to thrust our boarding passes into the attendant's outstretched hand dangling out over the check-in desk.

When we entered the plane, my mother's face finally relaxed. She was no longer in charge. With a curt nod, she graciously handed off her anxiety to the pilot and his crew gathered at the front of the plane before leading me down the aisle to take our seats.

I watched curiously while the crew made their preflight checks.

I was entranced by the ritual of it all. The attendants moved up and down the aisles like priestesses preparing for a sacrifice, muttering incantations as they pulled on belt straps and slammed overhead bins closed. There was a seriousness to the whole affair. I sat up straight in my seat and locked my eyes with the nearest stewardess. She was blonde and old, the lines in her face barely hidden by the layers of makeup she used to disguise her age. She was the high priestess, the head honcho. She directed traffic with her icy blue stare, controlling the cabin from the front of the plane without moving a muscle.

The ritual began. The priests took their places and moved in sequence as the high priestess moved us through the liturgy. I glanced over at my mom when they mentioned the life rafts. Her face was stoic, but I could tell the thought of careening down the slide of the plane into an inflatable tube unnerved her, which in turn unnerved me, my six-year-old imagination running wild with images of a fiery end in a watery grave.

My mother shouldn't have been surprised when I turned to her in utter panic as they talked about the possibility of an "emergency landing." All I heard was "crash landing." I was all too familiar with the concept. My father would watch the news with me on Friday nights, and on one Friday, I distinctly remembered the "breaking news" banner interrupting the banal banter of the anchor with images of a fiery wreck in a field. The image repeated itself in my mind as the stewardess marked our nearest exits. I had quite the imagination, and in my mind's eye, we never made it to the exits. My mom noticed my fear and grabbed my hand. She didn't say anything. All she did was grip my hand in a vice grip while she muttered a prayer. The prayer was as much for her as it was for me, she had that look on, and from the look she gave the stewardess, I could tell she was agnostic about their aeronautical religion.

We moved, slowly at first, and as we tumbled down the tarmac, I thought to myself, *this isn't so bad*. But then the rumbling started, and my small frame was pushed back into my seat as my ears popped, violent bursts sending my head spinning.

"Swallow," my mom said. "It'll get better in a moment."

I didn't have the heart to tell her that my throat was dry as sand, and at six-years-old, I swore I'd never hear again. But then everything went calm, the noise stopped, the popping ceased, and the plane reached its cruising altitude, cutting through the sky with barely a hum or a squeak. I was still convinced that my short life would end in a watery tomb, but the sudden calm was soothing enough that my fear slipped somewhere into the back of my mind, forgetting for a moment that we were at 30,000 feet.

The attendants came around with little gray carts, and as soon as I figured out that they gave out snacks and soda, any fear I had left dissipated into greedy glee as I watched the cart draw closer with cookies and cans of Coke.

Satisfied and covered in crumbs, I drifted in and out of sleep. It was about three AM, our flight was scheduled to land at six, and three hours cooped in a flying iron bird only goes fast when you close your eyes and let time slip by in your sleep.

We were headed to Puerto Rico to see my grandfather, Jose.

My grandfather moved back to the island after I was born. He moved to NYC in the '60s, leaving the island behind for the prospect of a better life in the states. There, with my grandmother, he raised my mother and worked factory jobs until he got his real estate license.

Things went well for a while. He sent my mom to college, got remarried, and set up his own real estate office with a Jewish man named Levi. Moving back to Puerto Rico was never in his plans. For my grandfather, life was all about moving forward. He was one of those pull-yourself-up-by-your-bootstraps kinds of guys who truly believed in the American Dream, in hard work, dedication, and the importance of education. He took pride in making something of himself. Born to a Corsican father and a Puerto Rican mother, his life began in poverty. His father left his marriage for greener pastures when my grandfather was a boy, leaving my great-grandmother to rear him and his siblings alone. Puerto Rico was a reminder of his struggles, the sleepless nights and empty bellies. Moving to New York meant putting all that in the past, and the idea of returning was a fate he chose to ignore.

Now, mind you, my grandfather was appreciative of his heritage, and he loved his people. But to go back was to leave behind the person he'd become—a self-made man. But life was cruel, and our plans were often ignored. As providence would have it, he'd spend the rest of his days on the island he so desperately wanted to leave in the past. A cruel twist of fate, stranded in the very place that he swore he would never return.

It was 1991 and business was going well. Bush Sr. was good to my grandfather and in those years, my grandfather's portfolio bursting at the seams. He'd acquired a beautiful property for pennies on the dollar. It was one of those old three-floor walk-ups, red brick brownstones. A fire had burnt out a good chunk of it, apparently, to claim insurance money (the owner mysteriously disappearing soon after). My grandfather purchased it for next to nothing and refurbished it with his own money.

It was coming along great, and with work still to be done, he had buyers scheduling visits. Boy, could he sell. He knew how to look at a buyer and, within a few minutes, he knew exactly what they wanted. With his yellow hardhat on his head, he'd sell families on the Brooklyn dream, a quiet neighborhood with easy access to the city and Queens.

On that night, he showed a young Polish couple the property. They seemed nice enough, but for all his showmanship, they wouldn't budge until he showed them the third floor. The house was still under construction and the third floor was far from being finished, but he wouldn't let that deter him. He led the couple up the unfinished stairs to the third floor. They made it up the stairs fine, but as my grandfather followed behind them, he heard a crack, and before he knew it, he felt the weight of gravity pulling him down. Through layers of wood, sheetrock, and insulation.

He described falling like flying.

"It's like flying," he'd say. "For a moment, you're free and everything gives way to the sudden joy of liberation. There isn't any fear, no thought of what lies below, just the feeling of freedom, the weightless tug of gravity pulling you under."

A beautiful lie before a sudden stop.

When he awoke, he was in the hospital, groggy, hopped up on pain meds with his wife, Irma, and my mother, Marie, by his side. The room was dark and his whole body tingled with morphine. They spoke to him, but all he heard was the warbling sound of distorted speech.

A few hours later, the doctor walked in. He was tall and gaunt. His face was too old for his age, weathered and gnarled like an old willow bending over the riverbed. He shuffled into the room with a blank look, the one doctors wear when they're about to deliver terrible news. The set mouth, the narrowed eyes, the distant stare, all signs that the news he came to share wasn't any good. My grandfather couldn't recall what the doctor said or how he had said it, he was too busy slipping in and out of consciousness. What he did remember was his wife weeping, my mother sobbing, and the doctor quietly excusing himself. It'd be days before he'd wake up, and even then, he couldn't quite understand what was happening. He was stuck in a morphine-induced limbo, floating somewhere between reality and a drug-addled, vegetative state.

When he finally awoke, his wife, Irma, sat down and told him what the doctor had said. He'd broken his back and he'd need physical therapy. At that moment, my grandfather saw the remainder of his life flash before his eyes. He was locked away in some nursing home, slowly decaying in a wheelchair like a dying plant, drooping and withering, wrinkles and gray hair falling down his face like melting ice cream.

But lucky for him, it wasn't as bad as they'd said. By some miracle or act of divine providence, my grandfather's back mended. He learned to walk again, albeit with a constant sharp pain that needed to be regulated. The doctor encouraged him to move to a warmer climate and to get a single-story home. By the time I was born, he was back in Puerto Rico, living less than ten miles from the town in which he was born.

The plane landed in Ponce at around eight AM, and as soon as we deplaned, the island heat smothered us in its wet embrace. The air was thick, and it clung to our skin and hair in thick, wet bands of moisture. Before I knew it, sweat pooled above my lips and the back of my neck, dripping slowly down my spine, leaving a wet blotch like an ink blot on the small of my back.

I can't stand the heat. At least during winter, you can bundle up and cheat the cold with a few extra layers. In the heat, there are only so many layers you can take off before you're considered indecent, and even after you've stripped yourself bare, the heat refuses to relent. It beats on your bare skin like a drum, oppressive and all-consuming, and your only hope is the occasional breeze or some well-placed shade.

Luckily, we had to go back indoors to collect our bags.

The baggage claim was packed with people speaking Spanish, most of them visiting their relatives in Puerto Rico. A few tourists were present, too. It was easy to spot them. They tended to be dressed in their Tommy Bahama best, their bags overpacked, shuffling nervously about as they looked for a sign with their name scrawled in black ink on a white sheet.

I didn't recognize it then, but I've always existed somewhere in the middle, not quite the tourist, not quite the native, the awkward in-between. Somewhere between otherness and belonging. I was too young then to notice the distance between me and the people walking past baggage claim. But looking back, I remember feeling disoriented, surrounded by unfamiliar sights, sounds, and smells.

A lady pushed past me to retrieve her luggage.

"Perdone."

I didn't move. I racked my six-year-old brain, but no matter how hard I tried, I couldn't piece together what she said. It sounded familiar, like an old song you couldn't quite place. I stood there frozen, as if all input had ceased to compute.

Then came the voice of my mother.

"She said excuse me."

My mother grabbed my shoulders and moved me off to the side. The woman looked about sixty. Her hair was gray, and she wore a baby blue dress made of satin. I watched her bend down and grab an overstuffed burgundy bag, the zippers holding on for dear life. She grunted and strained. My mother helped her lift the bag off the conveyor belt. They had a brief exchange. I listened in to see if I could understand what they said, but I understood nothing. The sounds were loaded with meaning, but their meaning was lost on me.

I hung my head, dejected, sad that I missed out.

My parents rarely spoke Spanish at home, and when they did, it was in hushed voices in quiet corners, with the occasional glance over their shoulders to see if I listened in. It didn't bother me at home. Parents had secrets. Every kid knew that. But being surrounded by voices speaking a totally unfamiliar language was a different experience, especially when everybody expected you to be in the know.

Our luggage passed around the conveyor belt. I rushed after it with a smile, taking pride in my keen eyes and quick feet. My mother followed close behind, and after we grabbed our bags, we followed the signs to the exit.

We walked down the pick-up line and saw my grandfather standing in front of his white Cadillac Seville, grinning from ear to ear, waving his hands above his head to flag us down.

My grandfather wasn't a tall man, but he seemed to loom over me. He was somewhere between skinny and overweight, his arms thin and toned while his gut protruded over his belt, giving him a bloated, pregnant look. His skin was light but tanned, liver spots dotting his balding head, while wisps of white danced on the crown of his skull. He had a thin, salt and pepper mustache that curled whenever he broke into a smile. He seemed to wear the same outfit every day; a short-sleeved collared shirt, beige Bermuda shorts, and black oxfords with white socks.

He waved us down, and as soon as we were near enough, he limped on over and cradled my mother in a massive hug. Tears sprung to his eyes and together they cried. They hadn't seen each other in three years, since our last trip to Puerto Rico, one I didn't remember taking but seemed memorable to everyone else involved.

"Como estas nene?"

I stared blankly at my grandfather while he waited for a reply. After an awkward silence, my grandfather grabbed my cheeks and looked over at my mom.

"You aren't teaching him Spanish."

"Papi, stop. He's young, he'll learn."

"If he doesn't learn now, he'll never learn," he replied.

My mother rolled her eyes and sat me down in the backseat while my grandfather loaded our bags into the trunk and got behind the wheel. The whole exchange went over my head, I was just happy to be out of the heat.

With our bags loaded in the trunk, Abu got behind the wheel and started the engine.

"Please, Papi," my mother pleaded. "Don't drive too fast, you know it makes me nervous."

My grandfather didn't say anything. He looked at me in the rearview and mirror and winked.

My grandfather drove like a man possessed. He thought speed limits were suggestions. We sped down the highway, cutting off anyone who slowed us down, weaving in and out of traffic like we were being chased. In many ways, my grandfather's driving was a product of his religious philosophy.

"I'm immortal until He calls me home."

That was the line he gave my mom every time he got behind the wheel. You see, my grandfather was somewhat of a religious man. Though, he wasn't obviously religious. His church attendance was erratic, his joking was crude, and you'd be hard pressed to get him to articulate the finer points of his faith. But he lived as if God was real. His religion was a lived one. He could've cared less about religious theory. What mattered to him was praxis, a set of beliefs he lived out. Among those beliefs was a strong belief in providence, a force at work beneath the surface of the world, orchestrating its unknown purposes in the lives of mortal men. In his mind, it was God who ordered the steps of the faithful. When my grandfather zoomed down the highway at breakneck speeds, he truly believed that unless it was his time, he'd be okay. I never bothered to point out that the Bible also said to honor authority, but by the time I was old enough to point that out, he was too old to drive.

The highway took us along the edge of the Caribbean Sea. The bright blue of the ocean was shimmering bright in the early morning sun. I watched the waves crest and crash on the shore in lazy repetition, dragging the beach back into the sea. As I looked out over the water, I watched boats dip over the horizon and out of view, disappearing off the edges of the map. Where were they going? I wondered. I imagined myself sailing with them over the edge to the uncharted worlds beyond the sun. I imagined that everything was brighter there, and more vivid, our pastels exchanged for new and vivid hues. But as the car slowed down and the sea faded from view, I was brought back to the real world, and the leather interior of my grandfather's Cadillac.

My grandfather took us off the highway and into a town called Yauco. After his accident, he settled down in this small, Southern Puerto Rican town a few miles from the city of Ponce. As we made our way through the town, we drove past the town square with its brightly colored buildings before making a left at the old catholic church next to the cemetery.

The cemetery stretched on and on. Rows and rows of concrete tombs jutted from the surface of the earth. The tombs were covered in tropical flowers and photos and the walls of the cemetery were covered in art. Faded paintings of Taino warriors dancing in otherworldly masks celebrating the dead and dying, denying the somber silence that dominated our funerals, as if they knew that death wasn't something to be scorned, but acknowledged for what it was—an interruption, a blip in the system, a brief stop on the road to the eternal.

After a few turns, we left the cemetery behind and arrived outside a creme-colored home with Spanish red tiles. The entire house was surrounded by a floor-to-ceiling gate that circled the patio. My grandfather took a small black box from behind the sunshade and clicked the white button that protruded from the surface. The iron gate that barred the way opened, squealing and groaning as the rusted joints fought to obey the controller's command, opening so that the Cadillac pulled up the ramp and into the driveway before the gate closed behind us.

"Welcome home," my grandfather said, eyes wide with joy as he looked back at me and smiled.

When my grandfather stepped out of the car with his hand on his back, my mother glanced over at him and shook her head.

"Papi, we could've taken a taxi."

My grandfather rolled his eyes and opened the trunk.

"Taxi's overcharge, and plus, you're my daughter. I refuse to let my daughter pay for a ride when I have a perfectly fine car and decent vision."

My mother looked as if she wanted to say something, but she didn't. My grandfather was loud and brash, he dominated conversations, and my mom had learned long ago to discern when my grandfather had made up his mind. Some hills weren't worth dying on.

"Now, nino, come, let me show you around."

I followed my grandfather through the front door, clutching my backpack against my chest in the way children do when they enter a new space.

It wasn't a big house. Only two bedrooms, a living room, an office and a kitchen. My feet slapped against the white tiles, but much to my surprise, despite the heat, the tiles were cold. Roosters of all kinds lined the walls, most carved from wood, but a few were made of stone, and one was knit together with thatch and wire. It felt old. The appliances were dated, and the furniture was covered in plastic. The only new thing was the tv in my grandfather's bedroom, a gigantic color monitor that lumbered in the corner like a large black bear.

After the tour, my grandfather led us back outside and onto the porch. I saw that the porch wrapped around the entire house. The tiles outside were patterned with little marble flowers and a jungle's worth of greenery covered the gate that circled the house. We followed the curve of the porch to the back of the house where an iron door sat locked with a chain. My grandfather took a key from his pocket and unlocked the gate, the tile giving way to the soft touch of earth. I wiggled my toes and watched as my pale feet were covered in brown dirt. Little bushes grew in scattered patches all over the garden. There were no plots or planters. Each plant grew wild and free, twisting and intertwining with the neighboring greenery.

At the center of the garden was a solitary tree. The trunk was short, and the branches were wide. Little green orbs hung from the lower branches, swaying whenever a breeze stirred the leaves. My grandfather ran his hand through the leaves and plucked one of the green orbs from its perch. He bent beside me as best he could and, with a knife from his pocket, cut through the flesh of the fruit in his hands. The green skin gave way to a bright yellow center, a brown pit suspended between the fruit's sunlit flesh.

"This is an aguacate, an avocado. I planted this tree after you were born. It was tiny, then, barely a bush, but look. After some love, care, and island air, it gave birth to some beautiful fruit."

Something changed in my grandfather's face as he spoke to me about his avocado tree. His eyes grew gentler, his mannerisms softer, and his face filled with pride.

I looked down at the fruit in his hands, the yellow pulp, and brown core, the green skin, which upon closer inspection was mottled with black marks. I looked up at my grandfather, his bare head dotted with liver spots. I laughed. The similarities between his spotted skin and the outer edge of the avocado triggered something in my six-year-old brain. My grandfather laughed with me. It was there, in the wild garden behind his house, that my grandfather and I first connected. He was no longer a stranger, the voice from the phone now had a face. He knew me, he knew my face, and for the first time in my life, I knew him.

We walked into the house laughing, my grandfather balancing a few avocados in his hands, while I held the one he'd split with his knife.

"Mommy, look what I found."

I held the fruit up to my mom, she beamed at me, and took a knife from the kitchen, and cut a piece for me to try. It was creamy and warm, and sweet. I didn't like it, but the smile on my grandfather's face forced the avocado down my throat, and from then on, whenever we had dinner, slices of avocado were piled onto my plate.

"Jose, ven aqui."

My grandfather's wife stood at the entrance of the kitchen with one hand on her hip and a hammer in the other.

Irma was short and her hair was cut in that pixie cut older women wear when their hair thins. I never knew what her natural hair color was, it was hidden underneath layers of unnatural red drug-store dye. She wore a sleeveless dress covered in a wild paisley print and her voice was sharp, as if the sound came from her nose instead of her mouth.

My grandfather had married her a few years before I was born. They'd met in a small Spanish Pentecostal church in Brooklyn. I couldn't imagine my grandfather at a Pentecostal service. He was never one for whooping and hollering. But after a few dates, they got engaged and were married soon thereafter. I didn't call her grandma. I called her by her name, though I never pronounced the "r," so growing up I called her Ima, and the name stuck.

Irma occupied a weird space in our lives. My mom's mother lived in New Hampshire where she worked at a halfway house for women. I adored her. Learning about Irma was confusing. I couldn't quite understand the space she occupied in my grandfather's life. As a result, I kept her at arm's length. Even as a boy, I viewed her with suspicion. But she was never anything but kind to me.

"Ryan," called Irma. "Go help your Abu outside, he'll need someone to hold the nails."

Abu was the name I gave to my grandfather at three-years-old, or so they told me. English being my first language, I could never quite pronounce the word Abuelo, and so after several failed attempts, I landed on Abu and refused to say anything else. Abu loved the name, and he proudly signed his cards to me A-B-U, happy to have a grandson to call his own.

I followed Abu outside and left my mother with Irma in the kitchen. The mailbox had fallen off the wall. My grandfather hammered a new one into place while I watched and held the extra nails in my hand with a determined look on my face. I wanted to impress my grandfather; I wanted him to know that I took my role seriously. We were finished in a few minutes. We proceeded inside and were met with a spread of bread and cheese. The bread was soft and sweet, and the cheese was hard and salty. My mother came from the oven with a pan of fried salami. I was starving and I wolfed down the spread put in front of me.

My grandfather made a sandwich with his and I begged my mom for another serving so that I could copy him.

After we ate, I started to feel sleepy. My mother picked me up from my chair and laid me on the couch.

I woke up a few hours later groggy and sweaty, my skin sticking to the couch's plastic covering. I'd slept most of the day and Abu and Irma were ready for dinner.

My mom forced me into the shower, and I spent the next few minutes shivering under a torrent of cold water.

Before I knew it, I was dressed up and sitting in the back of my grandfather's Cadillac with my mom. Irma sat in the front, fixing her hair in the rearview mirror. My grandfather got into the car last. He fumbled with the remote for the gate and I turned around to watch it creak open. The sun was low when we pulled out of the driveway and onto the street.

We took the backroads through Yauco, the last remnants of the sun painting the town in an ochre, orange glow. It was quiet, save for the rumbling of the engine, and the sound of coquis chirping away into the night.

"Coqui, coqui."
"Coqui, coqui."

The little frogs fascinated me, and I'd spend the rest of the trip in the garden searching the bushes at night for singing frogs.

We turned a corner and pulled into a parking lot on the side of the road. Golden bulbs hung above us, dangling like fireflies in the black sky.

We followed my grandfather into a restaurant, the music blaring as we opened the doors. We didn't wait for a seat. My grandfather led us through the booths to a table by the kitchen door.

"Sientate," my grandfather said.

We took our seats in the booth while my grandfather remained standing to wave down a server. A waiter in a white shirt and black apron spotted my grandfather and rushed over to our table, the busboy fumbling behind him with glasses and silverware.

"Jose, como estas?" Asked the waiter.

They carried on talking like two old friends. By the time they were done, our table was set with forks, knives, glasses, and a steaming basket of freshly fried tostones. I didn't remember us ordering. Food was placed before us, too much for us to finish. I was full. But every time I laid back in my chair with my hand on my stomach, Irma would say, "come, come. If you want to be big and strong like Abu, you need to eat."

My mom gave me that look, the one that said, do as you're told or else, and so I gingerly picked at the rice piled on my plate until everyone around the table was satisfied.

My grandfather acted like he owned the place.

He'd walk up to the waiter with a smile on his face and ask for additional drinks or would stop them mid-service to ask how they were doing. He knew everyone's name, and everyone listened to him. He had a mayoral air about him, that larger-than-life persona that pulled everything and everyone into his center of gravity. He was the center of the universe, the life of the party, and no matter where we went on our trip, it was the same. Irma jokingly called him the mayor of Yauco. I never found out how he knew all those people. But then again, looking at him, with his booming voice and infectious smile, I could tell why they liked him.

After dinner, I fell asleep in the car on the drive back home, only perking up when my mom mentioned an excursion to the beach the following day.

The next few days followed a similar pattern. We woke up, ate, and headed to the beach. After the beach, we'd go into town to frequent the little shops that made up Yauco's only shopping center. After a bit of shopping, we'd return home for dinner.

I loved every bit of it.

At some point, my father joined us.

His presence was a bit of a blur and I spent most of my time with my grandfather, following him around the house, helping him in the garden, or simply sitting with him while he enjoyed his coffee on the porch.

We'd listen to the coquis sing, while the sun drifted behind the horizon somewhere off in the distance, the island cooling as it grew dark, and after the sunset we'd watch the gnats and mosquitoes dance around the bulb hanging from the ceiling. We were perfectly content to sit and do nothing.

It was early in the morning and our flight was scheduled to leave later that evening. Our bags were already packed, piled in the corner per my father's instruction.

The room was dark, the sun barely over the horizon. I drifted in and out of sleep while listening to the low hum of the fan that spun above my head. I opened my eyes as the door to my bedroom slowly opened. My grandfather stood in the doorway, fully dressed with his shoes on.

"Get dressed, nene, I want to show you something."

I pulled myself off the bed and into a pair of bright red swim trunks and a black tank top that read, "San Juan" in bold yellow letters.

I followed my grandfather outside, confused, still half asleep, and a little bit hungry. My grandfather started the car and motioned for me to join him upfront in the passenger seat.

"Where are we going, Abu?" I asked.

"You'll see soon."

We took a sharp right turn onto a dirt road between two farms. A few malnourished cows meandered between the uncut grass as a farmer cut across the field on horseback, wearing nothing but cargo shorts and a red baseball cap, his skin brown and cracked from a life spent under the Caribbean sun. He looked like a centaur. Where he ended and his horse began, I couldn't tell.

The road took us downhill, and as the car dipped down into the valley, the road narrowed. Shacks of all shapes and sizes lined the way. They were built off the ground, standing on stilts, built to avoid the waters that flooded the valley during hurricane season.

The people there seemed happy. They sat outside their homes laughing, the men playing dominoes, while the women washed their clothes in big metal bins.

But soon the houses disappeared.

The foliage closed in around us. We were alone. The car slowed down, and Abu rolled down his window.

"Listen, what do you hear?"

I closed my eyes and cupped my ear. It was subtle at first, but as we got closer, the tiny whisper grew louder. It sounded like running water.

The car stopped and my grandfather got out. Without saying a word, he motioned for me to follow him.

He worked his way through the brush and disappeared behind a curtain of green. I followed, branches and leaves lunging at my face, and I did my best to beat them back whenever they got too close. The air was thick with humidity, the cool air of the air-conditioned car was a distant memory, but my grandfather didn't say a word. He pushed on, deeper into the overgrowth, following a path known only to him.

But that was my grandfather, always trudging ahead, guided by his principles, his sense of right and wrong. Rules he made for himself to make sense of a chaotic world. "There's always a way," he'd say, and most of the time I believed him. He always seemed to know what to do, and even when he didn't, he never let on.

With the butt of his cane, Abu pushed the brush aside to reveal a river running along a stone-lined shore. The water was clear and slow, the current barely noticeable, a lazy river if there ever was one. It was deep enough for me to swim but shallow enough for a grown man to stand in, and every so often rocks would jut up and change the course of the water, creating little divots and pools on the river's edge.

Abu took a seat on a rock and, leaning his cane against it, he kicked off his shoes and rolled up his pants. He lowered his feet into the rushing water and groaned with relief as the cool current massaged his sweaty feet.

I stood gingerly on the shore and grimaced at the body of water before me. It wasn't the water that unnerved me. I knew how to swim. Weekends at the YMCA had taught me to how to float on my back and doggie paddle in the deep end.

No, it wasn't the water. It was the unknown; the fish hiding in the shadows, the thought of sharp rocks piercing my feet. I imagined every possible result; being bit by a snapping turtle, drowning in the shallow end, getting pulled under the current and out to sea. I was an imaginative kid, an overthinker, even at six. Everything I did was a calculated move, a game of risk and reward. It paralyzed me, and when the other kids at camp went down the zip-line, I sat back and watched. I was the observer, too overwhelmed to move, too scared to commit.

"You can't stand on the shore forever," said my grandfather with a smile.

I didn't have the heart to look him in the face. I wanted to please him, but no matter how hard I tried, I couldn't work up the courage to dip my foot into the water. I was like a tree planted by a river, near enough to appreciate the flow, but too far to ever enjoy the current.

My grandfather got up and limped toward me. He towered over me, his head hidden in the glare of the sun, his body seemingly disappearing into the light. There I was, lost in his shadow, crushed at the thought that I'd let him down. He didn't chide me; he didn't say a word. He took my hand and led me to the edge of the shore. I panicked, thinking he might toss me in, it was something my father would do. But the push never came. Slowly, and trying to hide his pain, my grandfather lowered himself into the water. When he was submerged, with the river up to his waist, he told me to get in.

All at once, the fear slipped away. I kicked off my shoes, stripped off my shirt, and with my eyes closed, I jumped into his arms.

At first, I panicked, but then I felt his hands, and with a little trepidation, I opened my eyes. I was swimming, I wasn't thinking, I was swimming, and Abu caught my eyes, and we laughed.

Chapter 3:

2002

My father was a paradox of a man. He was both loving and cold, kind and stern, present and absent, a mishmash of the admirable and the detestable.

From day to day, you never knew who you were getting, the present father ready with a kind word, or the disgruntled middle-aged man who retreated into his study after a long day.

This trip was no different.

The ride to the airport was awkward. My mother and father were both painfully silent as I watched them exchange frustrated glances across the dashboard.

My father had woken up in a mood. Something about traveling always set him off. I think it was the lack of control, the giving of oneself to forces and phenomena beyond one's control. Knowing this, he controlled what he could.

We woke up early and rushed around the house as my father barked his orders from the living room, his command center. He was already dressed, a baseball cap, sweater, jeans, and those Nike sneakers that always seemed to be out of style.

All he needed was a stopwatch.

He wanted precision. Maybe that's why he became an engineer—numbers, angles, plans, and budgets—all things to be dominated and controlled.

Before I had the chance to rub the crust out of my eyes, we were out the door and flying down the Grand Central at a breakneck pace, my dad leaning forward in his seat, eyes locked on the road like a madman obsessed.

He usually was more relaxed when he drove. He'd play music, drum on the wheel, and sing along to the radio with that rich tenor voice he kept hidden. But not today, today was a travel day, and my father had no time for games on a travel day.

We were two hours early, and for a ten-year-old with nothing to do, two hours might as well be an eternity.

Our terminal didn't have much in terms of entertainment, most of the stores were closed, and the ones that were open only sold overpriced cups of coffee and those tacky romance novels that were only sold at rest stops, convenience stores, and airport terminals.

My Gameboy died an hour into our waiting, and my father refused to buy batteries.

"You've been on that thing all morning," he said.

I tried to argue. But my father wasn't having it and my mom, who knew my father's moods better than I, looked over and with her eyes told me to give up and be quiet. The rest of my toys and books had been swallowed up by the giant mouth behind the check-in counter.

My father told me to bring a book bag, but I didn't want to carry anything, and so all I had now was a dead Gameboy and a few nickels and dimes that clattered in my pocket whenever I took a step.

I sighed and stared dejectedly at the floor as I contemplated how to fill the eternal hour between boredom and departure. My mom turned to me, and as I looked up, she pointed out the people who occupied the terminal. Families sat next to silent elderly men, young women sat across from aging aunts, businessmen and college students sat shoulder to shoulder, each ignoring the eccentricity of the other.

The nameless faces were strangers with stories and lives all their own, sharing nothing in common but boarding times and destinations.

"Look, Ryan, at the woman over there, the one in the pink hat, what's her story?"

I followed my mother's finger to a woman in her late sixties. She was small, with sharp features, her fingers abnormally long. Her skin was pale from her neck down, but her face was tan, a thick coat of makeup creating the illusion of hours spent under an island sun. Her wardrobe was simple; a gray cardigan wrapped around a white camisole, khaki slacks hemmed above her ankles, and black shoes that looked like they belonged to an American Girl doll. But what stood out was the wide-brimmed pink hat that crowned her head.

It was anything but subtle.

It screamed gaudy.

Pink feathers stuck out from the side of her hat at impossible angles like a peacock ready to mate.

The hat was the only thing that didn't belong.

My mom nudged me. "Go on, Ryan, tell me her story, use what you see. What does she do? Where's she going and where did she get that pink hat?"

I groaned and buried my face in my hands. The game didn't seem fun, it felt like homework assignments, one of those workbooks my mom made me do on weekends to "get ahead." But my mother wouldn't take no for an answer, and with an hour left before our flight took off, I really had no choice.

I squinted my eyes and stared at her, taking in every wrinkle, looking for the hidden details that would give insight into the woman in the pink hat.

As I stared, I noticed little things that went unobserved in a passing glance. A small gold crucifix hung around her neck. It was faded and worn and had long ago lost its sheen. She also wore a watch. This, too, was gold, and like the cross, it looked old. Every so often she'd glance down at it, shaking her knee as she did so, glancing up at the departure list with her bottom lip trapped between her teeth. Her eyes were hidden behind thick coke bottle glasses and the shadow cast from the brim of her hat.

Details turned into plot points, and slowly but surely a story was born, cobbled together out of thin air, an act of sheer creative will. The story was simple, I was ten, and knew nothing of rising action and climax, but after a few minutes, the bare bones were there.

I looked up at my mom with a smile. I'd started to see what she saw in the game, and for the first time in my life, I learned that I loved telling stories.

It would be years before I'd decide to become a writer, but in that airport terminal, my mother planted a seed, a seed that would flower into a passion for stories and a love of language. A desire to see the impossible lurking behind the mundane, the stories hidden in plain sight, behind pink hats and coke bottle glasses.

"Are you ready?" My mother asked.

I nodded, trying my best to look inconspicuous as I gave the woman one final once-over.

My mother folded her hands and waited for me to begin. I took one last look at the woman in the pink hat, and after letting out a deep breath, I told her story.

My story focused on her hat. I imagined that the hat was magical, enchanted by a long dead sorcerer, and could cast a spell on its wearer, disguising and hiding their true form. The woman wasn't an elderly lady in a gray cardigan, no, she was in fact a beautiful maiden, a runaway princess trying to escape a doomed marriage. I didn't know then what a doomed marriage was. Maybe I heard about it on TV, or maybe it was a prophetic insight into what would happen to my parents in three years time.

The woman was secretly a princess on the run, hoping that her spell lasted long enough for her to board her flight and escape the ruined life that awaited her. The end of my story was greeted with applause. I smiled, feeling for the first time the thrill of an artist's approval, though that feeling was brief as I glanced over at my father, whose eyes were glued to the departure board. For the next hour we went back and forth, creating lives for strangers, trying our best to piece together whole stories from the little we could observe, the secrets they hid in the lines of their faces.

Time passed swiftly and before we knew it, the stewardess called our flight to board. We trailed behind my dad as he pressed his way to the front of the line, our carry-ons swinging in his hands as he struggled to pass our tickets to the stewardess.

My dad didn't sit with us. I sat by the window next to my mom while my dad sat a few rows in front of us. He had to get some work done, something about a big project he had to finalize. My mom didn't say anything, and I didn't think anything of it. But the cracks were forming. I couldn't see it at the time. A great rift was coming, and it would shatter the life I'd come to know. The gap between our two rows would grow into a chasm.

As the plane took off, I no longer felt any fear. I stared at the window in wide-eyed amazement as NYC disappeared behind cloud cover and the window gave way to the open sky. There was something about the endless blue that struck a chord in me. It made me feel small, not insignificant, but small, as if for the first time I realized that my life was but a cosmic speck on the grand scale of time. In some sense, that was what made life meaningful. We were vapor, brief but brilliant moments, occupying only seconds on the cosmic clock, and yet we were able to fill those seconds with life and color, symphonies, poetry, and families. Like fireworks, we burned for a moment, but our impact lingered on. Who was I compared to the infinite open sky?

None of this dawned on me until later in life, and I quickly closed the window when the stewardess announced the in-flight entertainment. I forgot which movie they showed, but like any ten-year old, I was a sucker for LCD screens and vibrant colors. I spent the rest of the flight with my eyes glued to the small overhead screen a few rows in front of me. I didn't have headphones, but that really didn't matter, the bright colors and frantic movement were enough to lock me into a trance. The story didn't matter, and I'd likely seen the movie before.

After three hours in the air, we dropped out of the sky and started our descent. I opened my window and watched the island of Puerto Rico emerge like an emerald from the ocean. Fuzzy green gave way to landmasses. Mountains, rivers, and low rolling hills popped into existence like pictures in a pop-up book.

The stewardess's voice instructed us to fasten our seat belts and put up our tray tables. I fiddled with my seatbelt and locked the tray table into position, feeling a sense of pride as I did so. Ten-year-olds have a keen sense of their age, double digits meant more responsibility, and teenhood was only three years away. I took every chance to show my parents that I was independent. I didn't know that innocence was something to be savored. Like all kids, I desperately longed to be older and free from the confines of my prepubescent body. I was tired of being a "kid." Middle school was around the corner, elementary school was behind me. I had made it my business that summer to grow up. In my mind, that simply meant being able to do what I wanted when I wanted and discard the trends that were popular amongst the younger kids in favor of those favored by the middle school students that I saw walking to the train after school. It's part of the reason I'd left my backpack with my toys behind. Where did action figures fit in the life of a sixth grader? I tried throwing them out to see if I could rid myself of them, but I couldn't, and even as I sat there trying to look older, I wished I had brought them on the flight.

The plane landed with a thud, and after a few minutes, we followed my father down the aisle and out of the plane. I noticed at once that this airport was different. It was larger, had more shops, and was generally brighter than the airport I remembered from our previous trip to Puerto Rico. For a moment I wondered if we'd even flown to Puerto Rico. Maybe we'd gotten on the wrong plane, and now we were stranded on some unknown island with nowhere to go. I ran up to my dad and pointed out this discrepancy.

"We're in San Juan," he said.

"Is Abu going to pick us up?" I asked.

"No, we're going to see him later this week, there are a lot of things to do in Puerto Rico, we're going to spend some time in the capital before we drive down to Yauco."

I was disappointed and I couldn't show my father. Instead, I smiled and asked him about San Juan and the things he'd planned. But deep down, I really wanted to see my grandfather. Ever since our last trip, I felt a certain connection to him. He understood me in ways my father didn't. I looked forward to spending time with him. He was the whole reason we came to PR, and as fun as my dad's excursions sounded, I couldn't help but think about the time I lost with Abu.

My father went all out for the first half of our trip. Once we arrived at our hotel, his demeanor shifted. He was laughing and joking, gone was the strict disciplinarian. The quiet and cold was replaced by booming laughter and warm smiles. As always, the shift shocked me, why couldn't he always be like this? All I wanted was consistency, and the constant fluctuation between distance and intimacy left me in limbo. My dad only knew extremes, when he loved, he loved big, and when he withdrew, he disappeared behind an impenetrable stony shell.

This trip put us into debt. Our hotel was top of the line, we ate out at every meal, and my father rarely said no to any of our requests. If we wanted it, he'd buy it. He lauded us with gifts and praise. I couldn't tell whether it was us he enjoyed or the fantasy of a perfect family he perpetuated on trips like these. Everything had to be perfect, he always checked if we were happy, and we didn't dare let him down. But the whole experience was draining. It wasn't real, and if it was, it was only temporary, the calm before the storm. Luckily, our excursions in San Juan only lasted about a week. We capped the time with a trip to El Yunque: a rainforest on the Eastern half of the island. My dad pitched it as a magical escape into the very heart of nature. I remembered being underwhelmed. The trail was packed with people, and the natural pool at the end of the trail (complete with a waterfall) was filled with frat bros on summer vacation, whooping loudly each time one of them clambered up the rocks and dived over the falls and into the pool. We dangled our feet in the pool before heading back to the car. All in all, we were there for about thirty minutes. That didn't bother me at all. I was happy to leave El Yunque behind. Whatever magic it possessed was now long gone, banished forever by the whooping of frat bros.

We arrived at Abu's house later the same day after sunset. As we pulled into the driveway, the iron gate greeted us and sprung to life as if on its own accord, opening its maw wide to allow us inside. We pulled in behind my grandfather's Cadillac, our rental a poor excuse for a car considering the antique's smooth lines and leather upholstery. Our rental was all aluminum and pleather, meant to be used up and discarded, a victim of capitalist obsolescence and American greed. I sprung up in my seat as soon as I heard my grandfather's booming voice over the idling engine. I swung open the door and ran into his arms, nearly bowling him over, the gap between us closing as I grew in height, and he shrunk with age. It had only been five years but both of us had changed so much. I was taller, my arms and legs too lanky to be considered useful, my face leaner, and my hair was short and neat. He seemed smaller, his paunch more noticeable, his back a bit bent, and his gray hair was noticeably whiter, little tufts of clouds dancing on his liver-spotted head. His old injury took its toll. He relied heavily on his cane, and though he tried to be spry, his movements were slow, and when he bent to kiss my head, I noticed his grimace behind his smile.

After we finished our greetings, we followed Abu inside to the kitchen where Irma prepared a feast. They usually ate early, about four PM. But since they knew we were coming, they'd waited for us, and while their normal dinners were usually simple, Abu went to the store and coaxed Irma into cooking more than we could possibly eat. The kitchen counter was lined with delectable goods, each more delicious than the next— arroz con pollo, bistec, surrillitos de maiz, tostones, and maduros, all hot and steaming, and ready to be eaten. I took it upon myself to make a plate and piled an inordinate amount of food on the thin paper. It nearly collapsed under the weight, but after some clever maneuvering, I took my seat and indulged.

"Perate, perate," said Abu. "Your food isn't going anywhere, and no one eats until everyone is served and we've said grace."

Grace. The word rolled off my grandfather's tongue and hung in the air. At the root of the word grace is gift, the idea that anything worth calling grace must be given. To say grace before a meal was to acknowledge this reality. The food before us, the people that prepared it, and the weathered hands that collected and packaged it, were all emblems of grace and thus worthy of our thanksgiving. When we're spoiled, when we have too much, we're prone to forget this, and like spoiled children, we rush past gratitude and are absorbed in our little worlds. But my grandfather knew better. He didn't grow up with much. He knew the hunger pangs of poverty and the responsibility that came with sharing all he had with his family. I, on the other hand, was spoiled, an only child of two college-educated parents who knew nothing of sacrifice. I took meals like this for granted, and knowing this, my grandfather refused to indulge my navel-gazing. After everyone was seated, my grandfather turned to me.

"Now we say grace."

The prayer was short and sweet. It was in Spanish, and all I understood was the amen at the end, then so be it that sealed the deal and sent our uttered words skyward. I got halfway through my plate before I started to feel full, but when I motioned to my mom that I was done, Irma wouldn't have it.

"Come, you need to eat, if you want to be strong you have to finish your food."

I gave my mom a pained look, but she simply motioned toward my plate, and like a soldier trudging across no-man's land, I slowly inched my way across the plate until a few scraps of onions and beans remained. That seemed to satisfy them. I threw out my plate and left the kitchen behind. The adults had started speaking in Spanish, and usually, that was my clue to leave, the switch in language signaled that the conversation wasn't meant for my ears. I wandered off into the living room and out the front door.

The patio was dark, island sounds filled the air, drowning out any sign of civilization. I sat on the hammock that hung between the house and one of the patio's columns and enjoyed the gentle sway in the cool island night. As I rocked back and forth, sleep took me. My eyes were heavy. I tried to fight it, but the air was too cool, and the rhythmic sound of the chittering coquis was too strong. I drifted off, unaware of where I was, occupying that pleasant space between exhaustion and deep sleep.

When I woke up, I realized that I wasn't alone. Abu was next to me, my head was on his lap, and his hands gently stroked my short-cropped hair. He hummed to himself. I watched him with my eyes half-open. I tried not to move. There we swayed, back and forth like waves gently kissing the shore before fleeing back into the sea. The soft sound of his hum was replaced with the deep tenor of his voice. The words faded in and out, and every so often he'd stop to make sure I was still asleep. The darkness hid the glare of my eyes, and when he was sure that I wasn't awake, he continued his song, and as he sang, the timbre of his voice reverberated throughout my whole body.

"Oh brillante estrella que anuncias la aurora. No nos falte nunca tu luz bienhechora. Gloria en las alturas al Hijo de Dios, Gloria en las alturas y en la tierra amor."

I woke up in my bed. The room was dark, save for the thin beams of light peeking through the blinds. The house was quiet, everyone was sleeping. The last thing I remembered was my dad carrying me to bed. I slipped on my chanclas and made my way into the kitchen, careful not to make too much noise. Outside, a rooster crowed. He was an old bird. He diligently patrolled the neighbor's yard and never failed to wake me up with his blood-curdling cry. But this morning I beat him to the punch. I rummaged through the fridge and found a roll of salami and a wedge of cheese. Balancing on a step stool, I procured a knife from one of the kitchen drawers and started slicing away until I had a decent pile of meat and cheese on my plate. It was impossible to grab a glass without making any noise, so I forgot the orange juice and grabbed a can of coke from the fridge instead. My grandfather loved soda, the way some men love beer, he always had cold cans at the ready. The supply seemed endless and there was nothing better than a cold can of coke on a hot island day. I took my spoils and made my way outside to the patio. I plopped myself down on an old wicker chair and proceeded to dig into the meat and cheese piled on my plate. My coke started to sweat. Mornings on the island were usually cool, but even under the awning, I felt the sun getting warmer.

I was halfway through my plate when I heard movement coming from behind the house. I put my plate down and followed the sound to the garden. In between the planters that hung from the patio gates, I saw my grandfather watering his plants. He'd sweated through his white t-shirt. He looked like he'd been working for hours.

"You know, it's not nice to spy."

Abu peeked through the gate and waved for me to join him in the garden. The garden wasn't as green as it'd been when I first visited all those years ago, and this was as green as it was ever going to get.

Abu wouldn't let anyone take care of his garden, and when he grew too old to tend it, it fell into disarray. I didn't know it at the time, but this would be the last time I'd help Abu around the garden. I look back on that moment and wish I'd paid better attention.

At thirty, I know nothing about tending plants, and I tend to kill even hardy plants like succulents. I regret not learning more from my grandfather, for letting that part of his legacy die, but at ten, you think that gardens last forever and grandfathers never grow old.

We finished watering the last of the plants in the garden and went back inside the house, sweaty and ready for some real food. My father was still asleep, but my mom was up and chatting with Irma in the kitchen over a pot of coffee.
 "Tengo hambre?" Asked Abu.
 My mom nodded.
 "Papi, can you go to the panderia and get us some bread. I haven't had pan sobao in while and I woke up craving it."
 "Si, si. I'll go. But I think I might need some help. Nene, do you want to come with me to the panderia?"
 I didn't respond, I ran to my room, put on my sneakers, and was by the door ready to go in a matter of seconds.
 Irma and my mom laughed.
 "I think he's ready, Papi."
 "Come on, nene, let's go for a walk."
 The panderia was a few blocks away, so we followed the main road until we entered a little square named after some long-forgotten conquistador. We made a left and walked until the smell of bread filled the air. The smell was intoxicating, and as we drew closer, all I thought about was the rumbling sound in the pit of my stomach. Pretty soon the panderia came into view. It was small. The walls were painted bright pink, and crudely drawn images of bread covered the walls in haphazard patterns. An aluminum awning hung over the entrance and a few old men sat outside in folding chairs, playing dominoes. It was busy. Men and women entered and exited at a frequent pace, and the only reason there wasn't a line was because there was no wasted time looking at the menu. They knew what they wanted, and after a brief chat with the elderly women at the register, they were out the door with a warm loaf tucked under their arms.
 But we didn't go through the front door. My grandfather led us behind the building to a backdoor held slightly ajar by a misshapen stone that looked curiously like a face when you turned your head and squinted. My grandfather opened the door, and we were hit full force by the aroma of bread. Saliva ran down my chin as my sense of smell overpowered the rest of my senses. It was heaven.
 A tall, well-built man emerged from the doorway. His musculature rippled under his stained shirt as he drew my grandfather in for a hug.

But his movements were gentle for a man his size. He wrapped his arms around Abu, careful not to put too much pressure on his back. When he pulled back from his hug, he grasped my grandfather's shoulders with hands as big as baseball gloves, dwarfing my grandfather under his massive frame.

"Compai! It's been a while," said the baker in a rich, velvet, baritone voice.

They spent the next few moments talking and laughing, going back and forth in quick, short sentences. They seemed to be playing a game known only to them, but the rules were easy to follow, whoever could make the other laugh the hardest was the winner and judging by the rib rattling laughs coming from the baker, it looked as if my grandfather was well on his way to victory.

If he didn't notice me before he certainly noticed me now. The baker bent low so that we were eye level, and with all the seriousness in the world, he stuck out his hand. The baker's hand swallowed my fingers in his palm. His skin was rough, stiff, and calloused from years of kneading dough.

My father used to tell me that you could tell a lot about a man from the shape of his hands. "Never trust a man with smooth hands," he'd say. "Hard work always leaves a mark."

At thirty, my hands are still smooth, and I still find it hard to consider writing work. Plus, I'd like to believe that I'm trustworthy. But then again, I work in the world of fiction, maybe my father was right all along.

"Yo soy Miguel? ¿Cuál es su nombre?"

I squirmed under Miguel's stare. The sounds were familiar, and I knew if I had time, I could muster a response. I racked my brain, but my mind was blank. Miguel seemed to pick up on my discomfort and without making a big deal out of my Spanish language skills, repeated his question in his halting, broken English.

"I'm Ryan."

"I've heard a lot about you, Ryan, whenever I see your Abuelo, you're all he talks about."

Despite my embarrassment, I couldn't help but grin, and when I looked up at Abu, I saw that he was grinning, too.

"Venga, let me give you the tour."

We followed Miguel through the door and into the bakery. The kitchen behind the counter was buzzing with activity. A middle-aged woman in a hairnet was busy kneading dough while a young man of about twenty pulled fresh loaves out of the oven. The bread let off wisps of steam as he moved them from the tray to cool on a metal rack. Miguel walked over to the rack, grabbed a piping hot loaf with his bare hands and slid it into a paper bag. I wondered if he even felt the heat or if years of handling hot bread had left his hands immune. He handed the smoking bag to my grandfather who handled it a bit more carefully than his friend.

"Buen provecho," said Miguel.

My grandfather thanked him and motioned for me to follow him out the back door from which we came.

"Abu, we forgot to pay."

"Miguel's a friend, I helped him start his bakery, which means we get our bread straight from the oven."

We arrived at the house with the bread still warm. My mom tore off a piece and bit into it. It was still hot, but she didn't care, she'd waited long enough. A few moments later, we were all sitting around the table nibbling on bread and drinking cafe, a satisfied silence occupying the place of conversation, each of us too enthralled by Miguel's pan sobao to speak. My grandfather didn't eat, he stood in the corner smiling, sipping his cafe. I looked over at him. There was a glint of sadness in his eyes. I offered him a piece of bread, but he waved me away and before I turned back to my plate, I saw the sadness disappear. It lasted only a moment. It came and went like a sunset, disappearing as quickly as the sun dips below the horizon. As if nothing happened, his eyes were bright again, and his smile grew even bigger, and in that moment, he looked like a man who had all he ever wanted. He savored the moment, the brief peace that comes with seeing those you love happy and safe.

Chapter 4:

2005

I couldn't sleep. I lay in my bed with my eyes wide open, staring out of my window at the gnarled branches of the old maple in our backyard swaying gently in the wind. I turned in my bed and looked down at the floor at my best friend, Ronald, snoring quietly, the air mattress squeaking every time he shifted his weight in his sleep. We were both thirteen, and puberty hadn't been kind to either of us. I was lanky and lengthy, my limbs moved at awkward angles, never quite going where I wanted them to. My upper lip was dark, and an awkward line of peach fuzz grew in to mark my manhood. Ronald was short, abnormally skinny, his head a bit too large for his thin frame, bobbing up and down like a bobblehead whenever he turned his neck.

We met in kindergarten. I don't remember why we became friends; I do remember that we quickly became inseparable. The summer before first grade, our parents sent us away to camp. It was called Camp Comanche. How the name of a Native American tribe from the Southern Plains came to be the name of a Christian sleep-away camp in Pennsylvania is still a mystery to me. But it was there, between the long hikes, the games of midnight manhunt, and the hippie choruses pulled straight from a sixties hymn book, that our friendship was forged. We emerged that summer like men from war, enduring tick bites, poison ivy, creepy counselors, and inedible food. We were bonded for life.

I'd somehow convinced my parents to let Ronald tag along on our annual trip to Puerto Rico. Our flight left the next morning. We'd spent most of the night talking about how we'd spend our trip, filling our vacation days with the pubescent fantasies of teenage boys on the cusp of high school. We were determined to leave with a story to impress our friends back at school. We imagined ourselves on the beach with beautiful local girls playing in the water in hopes to steal a coveted kiss. In our dreams, we were far more dashing and far less awkward than we really were, and while Ronald's Spanish was good, we hadn't quite thought through how he was going to flirt for both of us. But that didn't deter us, our plan was set. We'd sneak off from my parents and head to the beach by ourselves. There, we'd meet a girl or two, and with a little determination and a lot of luck, we'd return to school with bragging rights and cement ourselves in the upper-echelon of high school high-society.

What is it about boys that makes them yearn for glory? Is it a desire to please our fathers, or is it the constant teasing of older males that makes us feel as if we aren't men until we've secured for ourselves a female's desire, the uncles and cousins who poke fun at our virginal state, turning an innocent vacation into a perverse hunt for affection?

The next morning, we piled into a cab and drove to the airport. Once we'd checked our bags and secured some lunch (a Big Mac for me, a McChicken for Ronald, and enough salt-laced fries to punch a hole in a man's arteries), we boarded the plane. I'd begged my mom to reserve Ronald and me seats away from her and my father. We slid into our row and took our seats. I grabbed the window and Ronald was stuck in the middle. Luckily no one filled the aisle seat, and we were able to space ourselves out in our own personal lounge. We spent the flight playing card games, flipping through comics, and further discussing our plans. I gave Ronald the layout of the beach, piecing together my memories from our last trip to the island. We were so caught up in each other that, for the first time, I totally forgot about my grandfather. He was the reason for our trips. Our family could've easily picked a different destination, there was no shortage of brilliant beaches in the Caribbean. We went to PR for family; the weather, the beaches, and the food were the icing on the cake. But like most teenagers, I was tired of my family. Something happened after puberty, the people I once loved and admired no longer excited me. Adolescence had stripped them of the things that made them admirable. In my desperate attempt to grow up, to feel older, and free, my family was a reminder of my youth, barriers to be overcome and overthrown. I pushed Abu to the back of my mind. I felt a twinge of guilt whenever I did, but it quickly dissolved in a torment of teenage hormones. We made a pact, a silly, innocuous agreement to leave the island men. High school was coming, and every movie trope dictated that one couldn't start high school without their first kiss, and like the mindless teens in those nineties films, we were suckered into the game. This would be the summer to top all summers. Camp was a distant memory; we were men about the world.

But nature had other plans. When we landed, the tarmac was covered in sheets of island rainwater. The heavy kind that followed a hurricane. Great, wet droplets bombarded us as we ran from the baggage claim to the rental car. In about two minutes, we were completely soaked through, our shirts clinging to us like plastic wrap. My father turned on the radio and turned off the AC. The man on the other end of the airwaves jabbered on. I asked Ronald what he said but Ronald only grimaced.

"Sorry, boys," my father said. "It looks like it's going to be nothing but rain for the next few days."

I sunk into my chair and made a face at no one in particular. Our plans had been delayed, and with the rain as bad as it was, it looked like we'd be trapped in the house for the next few days. We arrived at my grandfather's house in a mood. Ronald, being a guest in a new place, hid his disappointment well. He greeted my grandfather and his wife in Spanish, and they were pleased with the idea that some of it might rub off on me. I, on the other hand, was standoffish and cold.

Even now, as an adult, I have the tendency to retreat inward, like a tortoise slinking back into its shell. I shut down and avoid all human contact, and when human contact is forced upon me, I do my best to let it be known that they're intruding on my space.

It was the first time I was ever rude to my grandfather. He came in for a hug like he usually did, but I rebuffed him, quickly turning back to the car to get my bags. I watched from the trunk as my mom gave him a look. If I'd hurt my grandfather, I couldn't tell. His smile didn't break. He looked at my mom and laughed. She shrugged her shoulders in return.

Everyone is a teenager once. But somehow, when we leave our teens behind, teenagers become a mystery to us. We forget what it is to feel everything intensely, for that is how teenagers experience life. Every action, every response, is dealt with as if it is the last, most important thing that has and ever will occur. The rain's interruption of our plans felt like the end of the world. Teenagers are apocalyptic in that way, the end's always nigh, the noose is always tight, and emotions are like volcanoes, pressurized and ready to explode.

I stomped into the house and threw my suitcase on my bed. I didn't bother to unpack. I laid there, watching the ceiling fan faithfully completing its rotations. Ronald followed. We sat there silent, too bummed out to reassess our plan. Ronald turned on his Gameboy. The electronic notes that came from the game merged with the sound of falling rain. I fell asleep, going over and over in my head what our vacation could've been if not for the blasted rain.

    I woke to the sound of a knock at the door. Ronald was still up, his face illuminated by the blue of his console's screen.
    "Come in," I said.
    Irma stood in the doorway. The smell of arroz con pollo drifted into the room. Ronald looked up.
    "Dinner's ready. Come eat."
    Part of me wanted to protest. I'd read about hunger strikes in eighth-grade history. Not eating seemed to be the best way to make my annoyance known. Ronald was a sellout, especially when it came to food. Without even consulting me, he hopped out of the bed and into the kitchen. I lay there for a few minutes with my arms crossed, determined to take a stand, to plead my case before God and nature. But the rumbling in my stomach got the best of me, and in the end, I decided it was best to put my strike on hold until I'd filled my belly.
    I went into the kitchen, made myself a plate, and grabbed a coke from the fridge. When I got to the dinner table, Ronald was already eating, halfway through a pile of rice with a liberal amount of hot sauce drizzled on the top. We ate in silence while the adults talked. From the inflection of their voices, I could tell they were gossiping. Irma always knew the latest family bonchinche. She'd gesture wildly with her arms as she told my parents who cheated on who, who had a secret drinking problem, and whose uncle was flat broke. I remember watching her spend hours on the phone with family to ensure that she stayed in the loop, and from the way she talked about our family, I swore we lived in a telenovela. Ronald and I cleared our plates and went outside to sit on the porch. The rain beat on the aluminum awning like a drummer without rhythm. We swung on the hammocks and watched the rain. For a while, neither of us said a word. Ronald didn't seem to be taking it as hard as I did. Maybe it was because he never really went on vacation. I knew a bit about what

was happening at his home, though I was too young at the time to process the gravity of what was really going on. Ronald had spent a lot of time at my house that year, and at the time I didn't think much of it. But after a few sleepovers, Ronald shared that his dad wasn't doing well. "Not doing well" was code for something that Ronald either didn't have the heart to share or was something he barely comprehended himself. He didn't elaborate and I didn't pry. I did know that a trip like this was a luxury for Ronald, and while I made a stink about the weather, Ronald seemed more than happy to waste away the day swinging on the hammock and watching the rain. My mood softened. We started talking and we forgot about our plan.

I can't remember what we talked about, but I'm sure it was mindless and pure, the kind of idle talk that only makes sense on the lips of adolescent boys. Sports, comics, and the occasional deep question that usually hung in the air unanswered. Tonight's question, "Would you still believe in God if you saw an alien?" I remember taking the question seriously. We were a Christian family, after all. In the end, I decided that God made the aliens, too. But Ronald was skeptical. Maybe God was an alien, at least that's what Ronald thought. I told him it sounded too much like an episode of Stargate. He agreed before finally deciding that aliens must have their own God, or at the very least know our God by a different name. Our theological dilemma was interrupted by my mom calling us inside for dessert. At the word desert, we forgot all about God and the gods of aliens. My mom had mentioned something about flan, and if there was anything more important than aliens, it was flan.

   Ronald and I woke up early the next day and scrambled to the window to see if the sun had broken through the canopy of rain that hung over the island like a funeral shroud. We didn't hear the familiar tapping on the aluminum roof, but we couldn't believe our good fortune until we saw sunbeams and blue skies. We wound open the blinds, and to our surprise saw the sun cresting the hill like a golden crown on a bed of emeralds. It was a miracle. The rain was gone. The roads were still wet, and water still lazily dripped from the awnings in slow, big drops, but soon, when the sun reached its peak, the ground would dry up. The rain would be a distant memory. We thanked God (who may or may not have been our alien overlord) and got dressed as fast as we could. Everything was back on track. We hunched over our cold OJ and stale bread, rehashing our plan and rehearsing our lines. After we hit the beach, we'd convince my parents to let us wander off to the empanada stand, and from there find a group of girls playing in the sand, on which we would work our "charms," which were pickup lines that Ronald had learned from his older cousin Eddie over Spring Break. Ronald worked on translating the best ones, though we hoped that they'd speak English. I especially did. I didn't enjoy the thought of Ronald flirting for me, and he didn't relish the idea much, either. When my parents emerged from their bedroom, we did our best to contain our excitement, and with as much nonchalance as we could muster, we encouraged them to peek outside on the porch. We danced in our seats, hoping and praying that the next words out of their mouth would be, "Let's go to the beach." Finally, after what seemed like forever, they returned. My dad was silent. He walked over to the coffee pot and poured himself a cup and didn't say a word. My mom retreated into their room. No one said anything. I was about ready to burst. I'd forgotten that there were seven days left to the trip, all I kept thinking about was the rain, and how it could return at any moment and ruin our plans. I was about to open my mouth, to do the unthinkable and say exactly what I was thinking, which as anyone who's ever been a teenager should know, is a cardinal sin, and as terrible as admitting to your parents that they were right. But before the words could leave my lips, Abu stepped into the room.

"Do you kids want to go to the beach today?"

Abu had come to the rescue. A mixture of excitement and regret turned my stomach. I'd been so rude the day before. I looked up at my grandfather and gave him a little smile, trying to say, "thank you" and "I'm sorry" all at once. If he saw it, he didn't acknowledge it, and for that I was grateful. No matter how old he got, Abu never forgot what it was like to be young.

Most of us leave adolescence behind and forget what it was like to live with every sense dialed up to eleven, with our emotions unhinged, exaggerated, and as sporadic as island weather. It's quite common to hear parents say, "I don't get my teenager," as if they'd completely skipped their teen years or had spent their teens in a self-induced coma. But Abu had somehow retained his memory. He didn't expect us to act like adults, he had grace for our teenage angst, and unlike most adults, he sympathized with us. He knew enough to know that it was better to legitimize our experience than alienate us further by holding us to the logic of the adult world.

We didn't wait for my parents to respond. With bread half-eaten and hanging from our mouths, we dashed back to our room to change. My swim trunks were packed at the bottom of my suitcase. I flung off my t-shirt and socks with reckless abandon, dressing my room in a pile of graphic tees, boxer briefs, and plaid shorts. I looked like a mad miner desperately hacking away at black rock for gold. I finally found them tucked away under a shirt that read, "*the man, the legend.*" It was a gift from my older cousin. But my parents didn't get the joke and I never wore it outside. For all my talk, I was shy. My body felt awkward, like a glove that barely fit. I never changed in front of Ronald, and even though I was currently excited about the beach, a small part of me dreaded to see my gangly reflection in the ocean waves. While Ronald undressed, I quietly snuck out of the room and shut the door to the bathroom. I slid off my shorts and put my legs through the holes in my swim trunks, adjusting in the ill-fitting mesh as it worked to lodge itself between my thighs. In the mirror, a pimply face looked back at me. I noticed all the awkward markings of adolescence, acne, crooked teeth, paper-thin biceps, and the outline of what some people called a mustache. The reality of the situation set in. There was no way anyone would be into this. The cool I was looking for was years down the road, and even then, I would never quite shake off that awkward kid in the mirror. I left the bathroom with my head in my chest. Ronald would have better luck, I thought. At least he was funny.

    We rode the rest of the way to the beach in silence. Ronald still seemed eager, but then again, no matter what was going on, that goofy grin never left his face. Abu drove my dad's rental while my dad sat in the passenger seat. He held his arm rest in a white-knuckle grip as Abu sped through hairpin turns and around vehicles driving the speed limit. Abu had insisted on driving us. Partly because he knew it would bother my dad, and partly because it had been a while since he'd been to the beach. You'd be surprised how little island residents go to the beach. My grandfather had lived in Puerto Rico for almost fifteen years, and he could count on two hands how many times he drove down to the beach and sat in the sand. For one, Irma hated the beach. The last time we went as a family, she made all of us vacuum ourselves with a hand-vac she kept in the back of the car. She didn't want a single grain of sand anywhere near her house. Plus, at his age, routine was king, and much to his chagrin, the beach never seemed to fit into the schedule. Which was ironic, because my grandfather loved the ocean. He often talked about his days at sea during the Korean War, the long hauls over the Pacific, the endless track of open sea stretching past the horizon. It was the only time he ever felt free. Something in Abu still longed for that freedom. As much as he loved his island, he also felt trapped by it. Injury had retired him here, chained him to the island he used to love, a place that at times he resented, especially when he remembered the life he used to have before he broke his back.

We pulled into the parking lot and found a spot right behind the little cabana that sold soda and snacks to beachgoers too lazy to pack their own. It was warm, a light breeze blowing in from across the Caribbean Sea, shaking the palms and kicking up little tufts of sand that swirled in pirouettes before settling down to join the golden ground below. Ronald and I kicked off our sandals and made a mad dash towards the water, wincing when we crossed the hot sand that separated us from the water. We hopped up and down, skipping and sprinting until we felt the cool relief of water lapping at our feet.

"Ten cuidado," my grandfather called. "The currents are rough this time of year."

For a second, I imagined what it was like to be pulled under the waves. Dragged out to sea by some invisible hand, fighting with all my might to make it back to shore, sinking to the depths, out of strength and breath. It sounded like a terrible way to die. But then again, isn't that the way we all go, dragged to our deaths by some invisible hand, out of strength and out of breath? Left to rot in the depths of some plot of cold black earth? All of us, caught in the same current, unable to make it back to the shores on which we were born, the womb we all seek to return to. The simplicity of childhood, a place we can only visit in memoir and memory. All our struggle, our desperate attempts to fight aging, the creams, and treatments and miracle cures. All as useless as swimming against the current. We only have one choice: to give in, to let it carry us, to let it take us as far out as fate permits, and then, when we're ready, cede ourselves to the reign of the sea.

We jumped into the water and under the waves, feeling the ocean rock us back and forth. We emerged laughing, content to splash around, and jump in time to the rhythm of the waves. In the water, we'd forgotten our plans. We were kids again. High school seemed like a long way off, and our urge to grow up, to leave our awkward, virgin bodies behind, receded to the back of our minds which each cresting wave.

My parents set up shop with Abu under an umbrella they'd rented from the cabana. My dad dragged over some beach chairs and set them under the canopy of artificial shade and was soon fast asleep. My mother pulled out a book, another sappy romance novel. She loved Nicholas Sparks. I never figured out why. Abu stood on the shore and watched us while the water lapped at his feet. I saw him wiggling his toes in the cool, wet sand, his eyes hidden by a large set of black shades, his smile as big and noticeable as it always was. We played and he watched, and we went on like this for hours, making up games, stories, and doing our best to impress Abu with our swimming technique. Eventually, we grew hungry, and we ran over to my parents, wet, dripping ocean water all over them. We begged them for some money to grab a bite to eat. My mom rummaged in her purse and pulled out a few dollars.

"Don't wander off," my mom said. She knew us well enough to know that we were prone to mischief. Our teachers had long ago learned to separate us on the far ends of the class to keep their classrooms from devolving into chaos.

But we promised we wouldn't go far, careful not to arouse suspicion, for now that we were out of the water, we remembered our plans. We knew that our hunger was our only chance to wander off and meet some kids our own age beyond the watchful eyes of my parents. My mom believed us, or at least trusted us enough to know that we wouldn't put ourselves in any danger. We thanked her for the money and wandered down the beach to the small shack that sold fresh empanadas and other fried snacks. Unlike the cabana, which was large and well-kept, this shack seemed like it needed a fresh coat of paint. The white exterior peeled in places, and the sign which once was painted in beautiful gold was faded and looked more like a piss stain than an actual sign.

A bell rattled above our heads as we opened the door. The smell of frying oil clogged our nostrils and coated our skin. It was hotter inside the shack than it was on the beach, the fan above us merely a decoration. If it spun, it certainly did nothing for the oppressive heat that had collected between the shack's dingy walls. But the appearance of the shack didn't necessarily speak for the excellence of the food. Though they would've failed pretty much every cleanliness and safety rating in the city, the food they produced more than made up for the ominous stains pooling on the cracked wood floor.

We left the shack with two empanadas each and a can of grape soda stuffed into the pockets of our swim trunks. With our empanadas in hand, we wandered across the beach along a line of pine trees that offered shade and cool sand to walk across. Our eyes scanned the beach for signs of life, but it was a weekday and early, so save for the occasional beach bum spread out under the sun, we saw no signs of people our age.

That was, until we heard laughter and music. We saw in the distance a small group of teenagers, lounging on towels and sneaking quick drinks from a bottle of liquor they kept hidden in the sand. They looked a bit older than us, about fifteen or sixteen, two guys and three girls huddled around a radio, laughing and soaking in the sun. The girls were beautiful, their limbs long and toned, their skin a deep, nutty brown. Black hair hung from their heads in delicate waves, curling this way and that, wet and heavy, hanging down the length of their backs. We did our best to look nonchalant, our eyes searching for something else to stare at, but no matter how hard we tried, they drifted back to the brown bodies dotted in golden sand. But then we saw the guys and realized we'd never stand a chance. Two years does remarkable things to a young man's body. Limbs that were once skeletal filled out with muscle. Facial hair, which was once patchy and awkward, framed chiseled jawlines and grew in full. They moved confidently, as if their bodies were theirs. There was no gait to their step, no clumsy movement. Their voices were clear, bold and deep, and lacked the crack that snuck into our throats when we tried to speak. We turned around and didn't say a thing. Getting dragged under water couldn't be worse than this.

    We spent the rest of our vacation in Yauco. Luckily for us, the next day, the rain began again, and we didn't have to return to the scene of our failure. We did our best to enjoy ourselves. But whenever we were alone, we talked in fear about high school, and wondered how we would be perceived now that we were storyless. We could always lie, but both of us agreed that that would violate some unwritten rule. It was better to wallow in obscurity than to ride the waves of stolen valor. Plus, if we by some miracle got girlfriends freshmen year, they'd expect us to know how to kiss, and since neither of us had succeeded on that front, we'd be quickly figured out as frauds. Lying about one's romantic exploits was akin to social suicide. We spent the last week resigned to our lot in life. At least we had each other, though I argued that Ronald's humor would fare him well. I was too serious, prone to being misunderstood, a loner at heart.

    We ate our last meal at Abu's favorite restaurant, where we ate mofongo to our heart's content. We went to bed that night too full to move. We shut off the light, said our goodnights, and drifted off to sleep.

    I awoke to Ronald shaking me awake. I rubbed the crust from the cracks of my eyelids and opened my eyes. Ronald crouched by the side of my bed.

    "What are you doing?"

"Get down."
"Why?"
"Get down."

I rolled my eyes and got on the floor. That's when I heard. Three loud cracks, like fireworks, but violent, and close. It was then I understood the fear in Ronald's face. I'd grown up in NYC long enough to know the sound of gunshots. But these weren't stray echoes, they were on top of us.

Crack.
Crack.
Crack.

I saw a puff of dust burst from the windowsill. Ronald and I lay flat.

Crack.
Crack.
Crack.

The sound of shattered glass.

Crack.
Crack.
Crack.

Silence.

We laid down and didn't dare move. We had been shot at. I saw the dust and plaster floating in the air in the moonlight. Shattered glass covered my bed and our heads. I grabbed Ronald's hand and, somewhere in the back of my mind, I remembered thinking, getting dragged under water couldn't be worse than this.

Seconds became minutes, minutes became hours, time stopped, the world stood still.

I never quite remember how long we laid there. It felt like an eternity.

Eventually, my dad burst through the door. He tried his best to hide his panic. He rushed over to us and patted us down.

"Were you hit? Are you okay?"

For a second, I thought I'd been hit. I'd remembered reading about soldiers who were shot only to notice when it was too late. I frantically searched myself for blood. It was dark, and I couldn't tell if the black of my shirt was the color of the fiber or a large pool of blood.

We were fine. Luckily, the bullets had hit above where we were sleeping. Abu was on the phone with the police. Red and blue flashed through the shattered windowpane. We huddled in the living room. Irma and my mom sat together on the couch while Abu and my dad went outside to talk to the cops. Apparently, a kid down the street owed a local gang drug money. The gunshots had been a warning. But the shooters had shot the wrong house, though I expected the kid got the message. It was over. The cops drove off and we all sat in the living room. Irma made us coffee. We migrated to the kitchen and silently nursed our mugs, the plate of cheese and crackers in front of us untouched.

    Then Abu started laughing, and when he laughed, we all laughed. The absurdity of the moment hit us. We'd all almost died. The bullet holes in the walls and windows were an inch or so away from where we slept. My dad's rental, the one he was so desperate to bring back in one piece, had bullet holes running down the passenger side door. We laughed. Anyone who cheats death knew that the only appropriate response was laughter. The sheer lunacy of it all left us in tears, our ribs aching and throats hoarse from laughter. We didn't go back to bed. We stayed up talking, eating, each of us telling our side of the story. Everyone laughed when I said that I slept through the first round of gunfire.

    It hit me. I looked over at Ronald and his smile grew as big as mine. We had our story. We would enter high school having survived gunfire. We'd exaggerate the details, the number of shots, the caliber of bullets, and our heroic response. But what good stories weren't a tad exaggerated? Plus, who needed hookups, we'd been shot at, and if that didn't give us the credibility we needed, well, in that moment we could've cared less.

Chapter 5:

2008

I shut the door to my room with a loud bang. I paced back and forth fuming, ignoring my mother screaming on the other side, trashing whatever unlucky bit of furniture was in my path.

That was usually how it went with us, arguing followed by shouting, which devolved into screaming before I stormed off and shut myself alone in my room. For three years we repeated the cycle, neither of us giving any quarter, always pushing, always prodding, always looking to get in the last word. We'd been close, my mother and I, but everything changed when my dad left us in the fall of 2005.

I'd started high school, and everything seemed to be going great. I had friends, I made the basketball team, and I even managed to land a "girlfriend" or whatever you call a girl you see for only two periods a day and for an hour after school. She was Brazilian. We'd met at a friend's Quinceanera, and after a few songs, we made out on the couch upstairs. We clicked teeth at least twice, but when you're young and pumped full of hormones, you don't seem to notice. I got invited to parties, and my position (not my skill) on the basketball team got me the hallway recognition I looked for. I was so wrapped up in the excitement of my newfound freedom that I didn't notice the cracks.

My dad worked later and later, often not coming home till way past nine. I'd lie in bed chatting to my girlfriend on the phone while listening to my parents duke it out below. They'd fought before, and I paid it no mind. I assumed that blowouts like these came with marriage and soon I stopped listening in. But the cracks grew bigger, and despite my self-absorption, I'd begun to take notice.

It all came to a head when my dad picked me up from basketball practice on a Thursday evening. He pulled up to the gymnasium in a car I didn't recognize, a black Mitsubishi, that looked fresh off the assembly line. I assumed it was a rental, one of those he used when his job called him across the country to negotiate contracts and manage budgets.

I opened the trunk, put my gym bag away, and climbed into the front seat. The car was silent. Usually, my dad liked to keep the radio on, alternating between classic rock and right-wing talk radio. But the radio was off, and my dad's eyes were fixed on the road. I grabbed my phone and scrolled through my unanswered text messages.

GF: "Are you done with practice?" (5:55 PM)
Ronnie: "Bro, do you want to go to Mikey's on Saturday?" (4:30 PM)
Mom: "Your dad's picking you up." (4:00 PM)
GF: "Can you come over when you're done?" (3:50 PM)

I shot off a quick text to Ronald before replying to my girlfriend. I turned to ask my dad if he could drop me off at Kathleen's house, but when I looked up from my phone, the words lodged themselves in the back of my throat. My father was crying.

I'd never seen my father cry. He fluctuated between stern and impossibly happy, but I never saw him cry, not once, that was, until that day in the passenger's seat of his black Mitsubishi. I froze. I didn't know what to say. I wanted to ask him if he was okay, but I couldn't. We drove all the way home in silence. Tears flowed from my father's face; I wondered if he could see the road. I thought about texting my mom. Maybe she knew what was going on. I thought against it. I buried my face in my phone.

"I can't come over tonight." (Sent 6:15)
"Party or hang out?" (Sent 6:17)
"We're on our way home. (Sent 6:18)

When I got home, I went to my room and lost myself online. My girlfriend called and I half-listened to what she said, something about going on a ski trip with her and her parents. She could tell I wasn't paying attention. She hung up. She got angry easily. I threw my phone on the bed.

We should probably break up, I thought. I hated it when she was like that.

I didn't shower. I fell asleep in my basketball shorts, on the futon I convinced my parents to get me in lieu of a bed. I left the computer screen on. It lit the room in a blue glow, and as the screensaver shifted back and forth across the screen, I tossed back and forth across my bed. My head filled with images of my dad behind the wheel, crying, driving into traffic, with me silent in the passenger seat texting away.

My dad never brought up what transpired between us in his car, but it remained present, an undercurrent of uncertainty and distance that wedged a gap between us. My parents also stopped fighting. While this might've looked like progress, I noticed the cold that had developed between them, and though all was quiet on the western front, the quiet had evolved into a cold war. A silent violence built upon itself, ready to burst at a moment's notice. It was about this time that I was introduced to tobacco and beer. I was on edge and my friends started to notice.

I don't remember who offered me that first smoke, but as I coughed my way through that first cigarette, I felt my edge dull, and after a beer or two, I knew that I'd found my brand of homebrew medicine.

I distracted myself as best I could. I slept over at Ronald's house and together, we snuck off to see his girl or my girl, or both if we were lucky. I couldn't avoid home for long, and when I was home, I boarded myself up in my room, trying my best to ignore the deep freeze that had settled between my dad, my mom, and me. It was like living with ghosts, or automatons, each of us going through the motions of daily life like everything was normal, but we all felt the weight, the tension. The rope was bound to break and break it did.

It was a November evening. The dusk was settling in as I took the long way home from school, walking rather than riding the Q1 to Francis Lewis Boulevard. Queens blocks are longer than normal, and if you avoid the main avenues, like Jamaica or Hillside, you find yourself on quiet side-streets lined with trees, walking past quaint, detached, and semi-detached homes, with rusting cars idly occupying the driveway. The walk added an extra twenty minutes to my trip. But I never felt the difference. My friends complained. I always lied and said the walk was faster than waiting for the bus.

"It's only ten minutes."

It was about fifteen minutes in that they realized my deception. But I couldn't help it. I loved the silence, the trees that bent over the sidewalk like the eaves of a cathedral, great spires holding up the purple sky while the sun dropped out of sight and out of mind. In the fall, I'd watch the leaves turn ochre and orange and imagine that I was in an enchanted forest from one of those fantasy books (a genre I read in secret to avoid the ire and suspicion of my teammates, who regarded anything literary with the stereotypical disdain forced upon young men with any athletic prowess). In the winter, I prayed for snow in hopes that I'd get the chance to walk home as it gently drifted to earth and turned the gray, cracked sidewalk into a footpath from the cover of a Christmas card. Practically, the long walk home allowed me to delay the inevitable. I was like a soldier returning to the front, hoping to stretch my shore leave as long as possible.

    That November evening was no different. I returned from basketball practice and took the long way home despite the blistering winter cold that had somehow slipped past the golden guards of fall. Like most Queens kids, I was wrapped up in a black North Face bubble jacket, which I unironically left open to the elements, letting it hang off my shoulders, caring more for the style it provided than the protection it offered. The wind howled and I tucked my head down and did my best to avoid the dirt the wind picked up off the ground and hurled into my face. I worked against the wind. My usual walk had turned into a long trudge into the biting jaws of the bitter cold. I zipped up my jacket till it clutched my throat, forgoing my look, while the weather turned sour. It began to rain. I never carried an umbrella or looked at the weather, and so I paid for my nonchalance with a healthy dose of freezing rain. Looking back, I should've known something was up. It was as if nature tried to give me a heads up. But signs only made sense in retrospect and prophecy was often written after the fact.

    I made it home soaked to the bone. I threw my bag down and made my way upstairs to my room. It was a teenager's room through and through. In place of a bed, there was a black futon shoved into the corner of the room next to a stack of books, a random assortment for a high schooler in ninth grade: Camus, Tolkien, Hemingway, Shakespeare, Homer, Heaney, Twain, Steinbeck, Yeats, Faulkner, and Lewis. A guitar and an amplifier sat opposite the pile, both dusty and unused, save for the occasional lazy plucking of a kid who never learned his scales. Beyond that, there was a desk, a dresser, a TV, and a chair. The floor was covered in clothes, some clean, some dirty, and in one corner there was an assortment of empty plastic bottles that seemed to never make their way to the recycling bin. I stripped down and threw my wet clothes onto the pile next to my bed. I stood there and took a second to look at my bare skin, still slick with rainwater, and took notice of its deficiencies, specifically the lack of definition in my lower abdomen. I did crunches constantly, but no matter how many I did, my abs never quite looked right. I was cursed to occupy the awkward space between fit, skinny, and fat. Too fit to be fat, too fat to be skinny, but toned enough to get by at the beach without much ridicule.

After getting dressed and dumping the contents of my gym bag into the hamper, I noticed that the house was quiet. My mom was usually home by now, and usually, she could be heard in the kitchen prepping dinner or moving about the house cleaning up the mess left behind by my dad and me. But the place was quiet. I left my room and searched the house for my mother. I usually would've stayed in my room and taken a glance at my homework, but the silence had unnerved me.

Our house was big, too big for the three of us. We'd moved in a few years prior, trading our home on 220th Street for a corner property on the corner of 94th Avenue between Jamaica and Francis Lewis Boulevard. My room was on the second floor, right by the stairs and next to the bathroom. My parent's room was down the hall, and a third room, an unused office, sat between them. The attic upstairs was finished and was only ever occupied when my grandmother, Abu's ex-wife, visited us from New Hampshire. Downstairs we had a living room, dining room, and kitchen, and below that, a finished basement where I set up a few couches and a TV. When my friends came over, we'd go down and spend the night playing video games and sneaking beers and the occasional joint behind the house, out of sight from the second-floor window overlooking the backyard. But mostly, I stayed in my room and left the rest of my house to my parents, who only ever really used the living room when the news was on or when someone visited from out of town.

My search downstairs came up empty, so I went back upstairs to check my parent's room. The wood creaked beneath my feet as I walked down the hallway, listening for my mother's voice. As I neared her door, I heard the quiet sound of heavy breathing. I hesitated. The room was silent. I lifted my hand to the door and waited. I felt like I was intruding, and my hand hung inches from the door as I debated whether to make my presence known. My mom was crying. I was sure of it, and my hesitation stemmed from that realization. For all her emotion, I rarely saw my mom cry. She was the bubbly type, anxious and hyper, like a gerbil spinning on a wheel. She was always talking, always frantic, and somehow always smiling. I liked that about her. She was my father's foil, a constant in comparison to his shifting moods, always moving between brooding and over the top joy. In this way, my mother felt safe. I always knew what mood to find her in, even if it annoyed me.

I waited as long as I could. I brought my fist down and made three quick raps on the wooden door. At first, there was nothing. I heard my mom blow her nose. I knocked again.

"Ryan, is that you?" She responded, her voice hoarse and strained, confirming that she had indeed been crying.

"Yeah, I just got home. Are you okay?"

Silence again. I fingered the brass doorknob, debating if I should enter or wait to be invited. Outside, a siren blared and broke the silence. Somewhere far away, someone needed help; an old man clutching his chest as his heart frantically beat against his chest, trying to pry itself free from his ribs. A young mother, alone, bent over in pain as her water broke and spilled onto the tile beneath her. A young teen, opposite a wooden door and the end of his life as he knew it.

I looked up. My mother was there in the doorway. Her face was gaunt and shadowed. Mascara ran down her face like black rivers covered in oil, painting her face like a Navajo chieftain from an old Western.

She moved to her bed and sat on the edge, hunched over with her head between her hands and her eyes locked on the wooden floor. I entered the room but stayed by the door and didn't dare move. I stood there for some time, watching myself watch my mother. I was aware of my breathing, the slight shift in my weight, the pain in my knee, the suffocating silence. My heartbeat, erratic, fast, and unnervingly loud. I couldn't move. I screamed at my limbs, begged my legs to lift and move, but I couldn't, I was rooted to my spot by the door like a sentry unable to abandon his post. Cursed to watch and wait till his knees ached and his eyes grew sore.

My mother looked up, as if for the first time remembering that I was in the room. She stared at me. Her face was empty. Like a statue's, lifeless and immobile. Her hair was matted and unkempt, her shirt wrinkled and wet with snot and tears. She looked like a small child, lost and alone, waiting for someone to take her home and to tell her that everything was going to be okay.

To this day, the sight disturbs me. There's something about the grown and the infantile that when combined create together a monstrosity, a mockery of age, twisting the adult into the form of a babe, useless and needy. It disturbs because, in the end, we become what we once were. Infancy foreshadows the dependence of age, that time when we'll need another to clothe us and lead us where we do not want to go. Youth is the illusion of independence; they see age as a means of escape. The youth believes that the older they grow, the more independent they become. But life's all about dependence and interdependence. No one's truly independent, even the hermit relies on the birds and the bees and the sun and the rain.

There in my mother, I saw what awaited me, a future of constant need, my life in the hands of others when all I wanted was to keep it for myself.

"Your dad's gone."

She got up and went over to the answering machine.

"You have one new message," said the machine in its robotic twang.

After a click and some silence, the message played.

"Marie, it's me. I'm okay. Well, not okay, but safe. I don't know how to say this, how to not hurt you, or Ryan, but if I ignore your calls any longer, I know you'll do something drastic like, call my job or the police, or you'll fly down here to try and find me. After seventeen years, I at least owe you this. I'm not coming home. I'm not happy, Marie, and I haven't been for some time. You know me well. You must've noticed, hell, I think Ryan's noticed. But we can't keep pretending. This isn't working. I mean, us. It's not working. I dread going home now. We're not working. Maybe it's me. I don't know. I think you're better off without me. I'm not coming home. Please don't look for me. Tell Ryan I love him, I'm sorry, tell him not to hate me. I know that's selfish, and if he does, tell him it's okay. Goodbye, Marie. Please don't look for me."

The answering machine stopped rolling. White noise crackled and popped before the machine shut off with a long irreverent beep. My mom was in tears. Her face was in her hands, and she sobbed, great big violent sobs that shook her body and the bed beneath her. I turned around and left the room.

I lay across my futon, eyes fixed on the ceiling, the splotches of paint and unpainted wall, eggshell white peeking out from behind Benjamin Moore's Chelsea Gray. I played the message repeatedly in my head until my sadness bubbled over into anger and my love soured into hate. I got up and threw my computer monitor across the room. I stood there seething, but when I saw my reflection in the monitor, cracked and shattered, disfigured by the chaotic lines that ran across the screen, I fell to my knees and wept. I cried until I was tired. I curled up in the fetal position on the floor next to my dirty clothes. At some point, I shut my eyes. I woke up the next day empty. No longer a boy. I was something else.

There we were, three years later, my mom on the other side of the door, screaming, demanding I go out and face her.

I truly think my father thought that we were better off without him. He fashioned himself a martyr, willing to give up the only thing he loved for the sake of those he loved. On the rare occasion he contacted me, his letters were peppered with allusions to his sacrifice. He would do his best to draw out his regret in thin, slanted letters that seemed to bend under the weight of the guilt that penned them. In his mind, I was free, free from his banal form of fatherhood that disqualified him from raising me.

I rarely responded, and when I did, I was quiet and passive, too tired to summon up the courage to put him in his place. This left my mother to face my anger alone. I fought her on anything and everything. She didn't hold back, either. Our anger was displaced. With my father's whereabouts unknown, we only had each other, and while we both loved each other deeply, we had no other targets for our rage. To both our shame, we became each other's punching bags, easy targets for our misplaced anger. Petty disagreements often turned into all-out screaming matches, me, the disgruntled youth, mad at the world, and my mother, barely holding on, feeling the weight of raising a young son on her own. We clashed over and over again. It was trench-warfare. The more we dug in, the longer we drew out the battle, casualties of a war we didn't start, a son suffering for the sins of his father.

That summer, my mother scheduled our annual trip to PR to visit Abu. I was sixteen, and the prospect of seeing my grandfather was buried under the disappointment of missing summer with my friends. As the trip grew closer and summer drew nearer, I pushed against my mom, begging her, demanding her to let me stay. She wouldn't have it. It had been three years since we last visited PR to see Abu, and our first trip back since my dad decided to disappear. I knew that she didn't want to go alone. My mother had become a recluse, rarely seeing anyone, opening our home to my aunt and uncle and venturing only outside for one of her three jobs. The large house that she used to love to fill with people was an empty shell. Occasionally, my friends would drop by, but even they knew enough not to make too much noise. We relegated ourselves to my room or the basement and would wait until my mom fell asleep to go behind the house, drinking warm beer, sharing our dwindling supply of cigarettes, and slap-boxing each other until we were too drunk to stand, or the mock fights turned into serious brawls.

I imagined that if my mom went to PR alone, she'd let me stay home alone, or at the very least let me crash at Ronald's for the remainder of the summer. I'd be free. Free of her and the shared trauma we carried between us, and I could spend my summer pretending that all was well in the world. My mother wouldn't hear it. I was going to Puerto Rico whether I wanted to or not.

Now I understand her reasoning. Who knows what kind of trouble I would've gotten into if I was left alone with a house to myself in New York City for the summer? But there was another reason, one I didn't see at the time. This would be our first trip back since my parent's split and her first time seeing Abu. Plus, she hated traveling alone. Whether I liked it or not, I was a buffer. If I went, the focus of the trip would be on me. If my grandfather tried to bring up my dad, she could use me as an excuse to shut the conversation down. She'd already done it with her friends. Whenever they reached out or tried to hang out, she would say that she was busy.
  "Ryan's a lot of work." She repeated that excuse often.
  If she had me, she was distracted. She could keep the world at bay and focus on raising her son. Going to Puerto Rico alone meant that she would be alone, alone with her thoughts, with my grandfather, alone enough to think, and remember, and feel the pain she'd put off.

When my mom put her foot down, she was immovable, a force of nature. She wasn't afraid to get in my face, and despite my show of force, she wasn't fazed. It was settled. We were going to Puerto Rico, even if she had to drag me there herself.
  I kept up my protest. I spent the flight with my headphones on and my iPod turned up to eleven. When we landed, I complained about baggage claim, about our rental car (a 2005 Camaro in a sickly tan), and about the cell service, which turned my texts into snail mail, forcing me to hit resend every ten seconds for my messages to go through. While my mother drove, I buried my head in my phone and lived vicariously through my girlfriend as she prepared for the first big party of the summer. A friend of a friend's dad had an apartment in the city. He was away on business and the house was empty. Everyone was going to be there. I tried to hide my disappointment. Eventually, she had to go, she was headed to the party, she said she was going to miss me. I didn't bother texting her back. By the time I got back, she'd be with someone new. Summer was short. Four weeks was too long to wait around for a guy you'd barely started dating. I put my phone down and watched the sunset over the Atlantic, dyeing the ocean with vivid purples and pinks, as the sun dipped out of sight and into the depths of the sea.

I woke up when I felt the car stop. Without opening my eyes, I heard the familiar creak of the iron gate working to move on its rusty hinges, shaking and rattling as it forced itself open, as if under duress and against its will. In the dim light of the driveway lamp, I saw the shadow of my grandfather lurking in the corner, waving at my mom to pull the car in.

He looked smaller, dwarfed by the floodlight that hung above him, revealing a slight bend in his back and a wooden cane leaning against the wall, discarded as we pulled into view. The man I knew was still there. His eyes were alive, bright and vivid, revealing the ever-turning wheels hidden behind his smile. But his limbs were no longer limber. He moved slowly and methodically, like a tortoise sliding across the sand, his cane tapping out his path as he walked across the tile. He was thinner, too. The bulge around his midriff was gone, his arms were thin and wiry, and his skin was translucent, revealing a network of blue veins darting this way and that, protruding from the surface like little blue hills in a snowstorm.

"Come here, mijo, give your Abuelo a hug." His voice was still loud and deep, ringing out despite his shrunken frame.

I walked up to him, and, for the first time, I realized that I towered over him. When I hugged him, his head was in my chest, the way my head used to sink into his, his ear nestled against my sternum as if listening for the faint sound of a pulse. His body was bony and sharp, and I felt that if I were to hug him any harder, something would snap. I pulled away and looked down at him, taking him in like he was a stranger, and we were meeting for the first time. In many ways we were. I was tall and strong, full of life and vigor, my arms firm, my chest filled out, and my face covered in a thin layer of hair. I had drunk my first beer, kissed my first girl, I'd fought with friends, made up with enemies. I'd lived, I'd lost. The innocence of boyhood was gone. In two years, I'd be going to college. Three years changed a whole lot. We'd changed. The bond we shared was a bond shared by a boy and his Abuelo. But we were different, and as I stepped away, I wondered if our bond survived the change.

You see, in those years I rarely spoke to Abu. When he would call, I stayed on the phone for less than a few minutes before quickly handing it back to my mother. Pretty soon, I stopped getting on the phone all together.

I don't know why. But seeing him there, hunched over in the light of his driveway, I realized that the gap between us was larger than I thought.

Part of me wanted to bridge it, to find a new way for us to reconnect, but another part of me refused. I'd looked up to my father, and now that he was gone, I had a deep mistrust for paternal male figures. Men like Abu, my teachers, and coaches were lumped in with my father, and when they tried to reach out, I put up a wall. I figured they would eventually let me down, and I didn't want to give them a chance. When Abu placed his hand on my shoulder, I tensed up and extricated myself from his grip. I didn't stop to look back, but I knew that there would be a pained look on his face, and when I was in my room alone, I sat up in bed and cried, feeling alone in a place that once felt like home.

I spent the rest of the trip by myself. For the first time, I was allowed to wander around Yauco alone. I woke up in the mornings, ate, downed a cup of coffee, and walked a mile or so to the local basketball courts. The guys who played there were about my age, and with my terrible Spanish and their bare-bones knowledge of English, we managed to get a few games together. I played until my tank-top stuck my chest and sweat ran down my face and stung my eyes. When the sun reached its peak, I jogged on over to a stand on the side of the road that sold snacks and soda and sat under the shade of a palm drinking grape soda and eating plantain chips. I went home, showered, and waited for the sun to dip a bit. When the air grew cool, I walked to the square at the center of town and watched as people convened to dance salsa and drink beer in the open air. I'd snag a few beers for myself from a guy who sold them out of a cooler and didn't care to ask for ID before sitting on a bench by myself. Two or three beers in, I felt confident enough to ask a girl to dance. I was a terrible dancer. My feet couldn't follow a beat to save my life. But I used that to my advantage. With the best Spanglish I could muster, I'd walk up to a girl and explain that I was from NYC and that I wanted to learn to dance. They almost always said yes, and for the next hour or so, I did my best not to step on their feet. Sometimes we kissed, but never more than that. When it got late, I walked home, heated up the leftovers and went to bed.

    I barely saw Abu, Irma, or my mom for the first few days, and when I did, it was in passing. When they went out, to the beach or to Ponce to eat, I declined and stayed behind. When I was alone, I tried to call my friends. I got a signal in the kitchen, so I would sit on the counter with my head cocked while my friends updated me about life back in the city. People were breaking up, new friends were being made, adventures were being had, and I missed out on all of it. Eventually, I stopped calling. I was missing out on too much and it was worse to hear about it than to not hear about it at all.

Two weeks in, my girlfriend texted to let me know that she was breaking up with me. I knew it was coming, summer relationships don't last, especially when you're miles away. She apologized and admitted that she'd met someone at a party. I responded with a curt "okay" and went about my day. I wasn't in love and wouldn't be in love for some time. Love was synonymous with connection, and at the time, I was too scared and too bruised to connect with anyone.

As the trip ended, Abu suggested that we go to church. The church that he'd helped start was celebrating its twentieth anniversary and he wanted us to come to the anniversary service. The next day, my mom took me to the mall in Ponce to get some church-appropriate clothes. We left the mall with a cheap black suit, the polyester kind that scratched at your skin and shrunk after two or three trips to the dry cleaners, and a pair of Payless brand loafers that squeaked and squawked every time you moved your feet.

That Sunday was hot and humid as if the whole sky was wrapped in a thick, heavy, wet blanket. When I woke up, perspiration had already pooled on the surface of my skin. I took a cold shower, but its relief was brief, and as I put on my suit, I felt myself suffocating. It was like wearing a sauna. The black suit absorbed the heat of the sun and trapped me in a polyester torture chamber. I was miserable. I tried putting on my tie. I fumbled with the knot, pulling the tie this way and that, looping and unlooping until in frustration I tossed the tie to the side of my bed.

There was a knock at the door. I turned to see who it was. Abu stood in the door frame. He wore a loose white shirt with brown patterns snaking up and around the collar and a pair of khaki slacks that seemed a bit too big for him now that he'd lost some weight.

"Do you need help?" He asked, motioning to the tie curled up on the floor like a snake resting in the sun.

I reached down and picked it up. He motioned for me to sit down and took the tie from my hands. He flipped up my collar and slid the tie around my neck. He passed the tie over itself and through the knot and secured it tightly around my neck. Before I could say thank you, he undid it and did it again, passing the tie over and under and over again. He took my hands and, like a puppeteer, guided them through the motions, over and under, and over again. He stepped back and with the warmth of his hands still present on mine, I took the tie and did it myself, passing it through the knot and tightening it enough to give myself a little breathing room. Abu stood back and beamed with pride.

"Te estás convirtiendo en un hombre ante mis propios ojos."

"What was that, Abu?" I replied.

"Nothing, mijo."

Abu turned around and walked back toward the open door, but before he walked out into the hall, he turned back and paused. We hadn't talked about my dad; he didn't ask, and I didn't share. There was nothing to say. But at that moment, all was said that needed to be said, nothing more, nothing less. He took one last look at the knot in my tie and smiled before meeting my eyes with his. They were wet, and tears danced on the edge of eyelids like a tightrope walker suspended between two points. He went to open his mouth, then as if he thought better of it, he turned around and walked out the door, and as I bent down to put on my shoes, I heard his voice in the hallway, small, yet powerful.

"I'm proud of you."

That was all he said, and it was all I needed to hear.

Chapter 6:

2010

I met her when I was seventeen. She was short and fair, with a pixie face surrounded by waves of curly hair. She had a birthmark above her upper lip, and when she talked it bobbed up and down, drawing my eyes to her lips, which were pink and plump and framed the whites of teeth when she smiled. That big, open smile that could light up a room with ease. She was a friend of a friend, and I was enamored with her from the moment we met.

We were introduced at a birthday party. While I played the extrovert at school, deep down I was your stereotypical introvert. I preferred books and quiet rooms to the loud parties my friends dragged me to, and while the need to keep up appearances kept me at the party, I often found myself in a corner quietly sipping beer and smoking a cigarette. My friend Janiece's birthday was no different. It was a sit-down dinner at one of those restaurants that served overpriced food and justified it with fairy lights in the rafters and that urban-chic decor that tries its best to imitate Williamsburg in the early 2000s, and now hangs in every small town with a "Main Street." I walked through the doors and through the dim seating area to a private room in the back, hidden behind two gray barn doors. I knew no one. My friend Janiece was surrounded by a ragtag collection of theater kids, short and tall, gangly and gorgeous, all trying to sync up in harmony to a song I didn't know from a show I'd never seen. The only person I recognized was her boyfriend. He was tall and muscular, with a clean-shaven head and armful of tattoos, one of which spelled out his name, as if he were prone to amnesia and needed the constant reminder. I greeted Janiece and wandered over to where Brian was standing. I was never good at small talk. I found the whole concept annoying, the posturing, the feigning interest, the banal questions and answers which were always the same and never changed. After weather and sports, I was all out of things to say, and if the person I was speaking with failed to continue the conversation, I usually clamed up and awkwardly walked away. Luckily for me, Brian wasn't the talkative type. He was a military, or at least he wanted to be, and after a brief exchange, which consisted of a greeting and a brief comment on the state of the NY Mets, I turned around to find my seat at the table.

She sat across from me in a black dress that hung from her shoulders and hugged her petite frame. She quietly stirred her drink, looking off into the distance as if she could see something hidden in the red brick on the far side of the room.

"How do you know Janiece?" I asked.

She looked up. Our eyes met. She seemed guarded, her arms close, her eyes narrowing in response to my gaze, but then she relaxed. Her arms dropped to the table and her eyes widened to reveal a deep hazel brown, light and earthy against the white of her eyes.

"If you must know, I grew up with her. The real question is, how do you know her?" She asked.

"I dated her best friend," I replied.

She looked at me, amused. "I don't remember dating you, so I guess that means you shacked up with someone else."

"Yeah, her name is..."

"Don't tell me," she interrupted. "Let me guess?"

We spent the rest of the night together, bantering back and forth, subtly flirting, testing the limits of the other. We were like fencers, lunging and parrying, each wary of the other, both of us trying to land the fatal blow. She was all energy and sparkle, a lightning bolt in a woman's body, witty, cheerful, and always laughing. I was her opposite, brooding, sarcastic, and pompous. We couldn't get enough of each other, and when the party moved from the restaurant to someone's house, we stayed upstairs and talked on the couch while the theater kids did karaoke downstairs. By the end of the night, we'd exchanged numbers. I walked her to the door, and before she turned to leave, she placed a kiss on my cheek.

As the party died down, Janiece came upstairs to grab a soda from the fridge as I was preparing to leave.

"Thank you for coming."

"Of course, I hope you like it," I said, pointing to the gift I left for her on the dining room table.

She walked over and examined the wrapping paper and shook it in mock-excitement. "Thank you, I'm sure I will."

We hugged. I put on my leather jacket and straightened my shirt.

"By the way."

I turned to face Janiece. She had a look of concern on her face, the look she usually gave me before I did something incredibly stupid.

"Don't pretend that I didn't see you flirting with Morgan all night."

I bowed my head and blushed like a small child who'd been caught with his hand in the cookie jar.

"You saw that, did you? Listen, I'm not saying that it's anything, but we had fun tonight."

"I know, I could tell. But be careful, Ryan. I love her, and I think you'd be great for her, just watch it. She doesn't know what she wants. I'd hate to see you get hurt."

I rolled my eyes. Janiece was always protective of me. Maybe because she was the only one who saw past my bravado, my brooding stare. Out of all my friends, she saw me for who I was: a hurt, scared, and angry kid who wanted to be loved. But I was self-destructive, and too often I shrugged off her advice only to land in the exact spot she said I would. That night was no different. I ignored her warning, and a few days later, after I'd waited the appropriate amount of time (four to five days to be exact, any shorter seems desperate, any longer seems cruel), I called Morgan, and when she picked up the phone, I knew I was in trouble.

We spent the next year dancing around each other. Doing the will they, won't they, teasing and flirting until the sexual tension grew almost unbearable. We toed the line between friend and lover like a demilitarized zone, edging ourselves to all-out war before turning back to stare at each other across that barbwire divide. For my part, I was falling madly in love. Though whenever I had the opportunity to say as much, I held back, afraid that any confession on my part would bring an end to the pseudo-sexual dance we were doing; the late-night texts, the suggestive remarks, the near-miss kisses, and the hours spent playing at lovers pretending to be friends. She never said a word, and we kept up our game until being near each other grew unbearable and the same tension that used to fill us with frenetic energy now left us feeling frustrated.

It was my senior year and prom was around the corner. I went to a small, religious, private school where dating was something like an inbred monarchy. Everyone slept with everyone, and by senior year, couples had been firmly established and anyone left single, you'd either already hooked up with or had hooked up with one of your friends, making dating them impossible. By senior year, I'd all but exhausted my dating prospects at school, which meant my date would have to be an outsider. Granted, I wasn't all too thrilled for prom. In my mind, it was a waste of an evening. School-sanctioned parties were always terrible, the DJs were always out of date, and the dancing was limited to jumping up and down and swaying awkwardly when they played that one slow song and allowed the genders within three feet of each other. But my sense of finality weighed out my misgivings. High school was ending, a chapter was ending, and despite my loathing for parties, especially prom, I knew that I'd regret not going. At the same time, prom was the perfect opportunity for me to tell Morgan how I felt. We both could care less about the pomp and circumstance, but the invitation to attend an event as a couple would finally bring everything out into the open, and if we spent the night pretending to be a couple, we might get a taste for the real thing.

 I had it in my head to ask her on her birthday. I had no plan and there were no "promposals" back then. But it seemed like the perfect time to ask. At least there would be alcohol and a little liquid courage never hurt.

 I heard the music from down the block. The bass thumped like a heartbeat, shaking the neighborhood. The sound of partygoers cut through the music like a commentary track, drowning out the lyrics in a pool of indistinguishable voices. I went through the front door and dropped off my gift on the kitchen counter, where a pile of colored bags and badly wrapped boxes were haphazardly strewn. Morgan loved elephants, especially the ones depicted in Indian art, dressed in royal regalia and fitted with gold bands on their tusks. Her room was home to a tiny collection of elephant-related memorabilia, posters, statues, and the occasional stuffed toy. It was one of the quirky things I liked about her. It certainly wasn't sexy, but that was the point, her quirkiness was a reminder that she was infinitely more interesting than her sex appeal. Sure, she was beautiful, but I was on the cusp of adulthood, and sex had taken a back seat to personality, character. It was possible to have sex with someone you found utterly boring. It was impossible to fall in love with someone who bored you. I bought her a little elephant hand-hewn from crystal. It was about the size of her palm and sparkled when you held it up to the light. It served no practical purpose, except maybe as a paperweight, but its beauty outweighed its practicality. Plus, who liked pragmatic gifts; sweaters, socks, things defined by their utility, their ability to be made useful and thus valuable? Weren't the best gifts valuable in and of themselves, beyond their monetary worth? Wasn't that why our parents loved handmade cards, put together with nothing but construction paper, dry macaroni, and glitter? The best things in life existed for themselves. The good, the true, and the beautiful were good, and true, and beautiful because they were ultimate. What was ultimate was ultimately transcendent, a brief glimpse of the divine, the truly real bound up in the seemingly useless, a crystal elephant, a work of art, a whispered prayer.

I made my way through the living room and through the screen door that led to the patio. The redwood was draped in white string lights and red cups littered the railing. Outside, in her backyard, people were dancing, their bodies moving in sync to the steady growl of the bass, sweat dripping as they rubbed up against each other like animals in heat. I moved through the crowd, pushing past the writhing bodies, and made my way to the far end of the backyard where a red cooler lay propped up against a tree, its white cover carelessly tossed to the side. Beer bobbed up and down in the melted ice. I stuck my hand into the freezing waters and fished past the Smirnoff Ice for a green bottle of Heineken. I popped the top with the bottle opener that swam around in the water and took a long, deep swig. The carbonation stung my throat and twisted my empty stomach. I forced myself to keep drinking, and when the bottle was empty, grabbed another beer. As I was removing the bottle cap, I saw Morgan on the patio. She wore a cropped shirt and denim shorts that hugged the tops of her thighs. Her hair was shorter, having recently cut it, and she wore a set of glow sticks around her neck and head like a pagan princess ready for sacrificial slaughter. I made my back through the crowd and made eye contact with Morgan. Her eyes lit up and from the slight sway in her movements, I could tell she was somewhere between tipsy and drunk.

"You came!" She ran up to me and wrapped her arms around me and pressed her face against my chest.

"Of course," I said. "I wouldn't miss this for the world, and by the way, happy birthday."

She beamed. "What did you get me?"

I shrugged and she pouted in mock disappointment.

"You'll find out soon enough. Plus, it would only spoil the surprise."

"Fine," she replied. "But remember you said that when it's your birthday and you're begging me to tell you what I got you."

I rolled my eyes and wrapped my arm around her shoulder. She nestled into the crevice on my arm and leaned her head against my chest. We stood there like that for some time, watching her friends dance from our little world atop the patio. It was the perfect moment to ask her. But I relented. I relished the feeling of her head against me, the warmth of her body, the steady rise and fall of her chest as she breathed, the goosepimples on her exposed stomach, her auburn curls. If I spoke, the spell would break, our moment would be lost, and every time I opened my mouth to ask, the words wouldn't come. She stiffened as if suddenly remembering something, like a rabbit in a clearing who hears the crack of a twig under the hunter's boots. She extricated herself from my arm. She looked at me, her face pained, a mixture of regret, longing, and betrayal. It quickly disappeared and was replaced with a thin smile that barely covered up all she tried to hide. It was the first time she felt distant, but I brushed it off. She said she was going to grab a drink and dance with her girlfriends. I obliged and leaned on the railing while she disappeared into the sweaty throng below.

    Two hours later, I looked for Morgan. I was ready to ask her. I was four beers in, and the buzz was enough to give me the courage to leave my perch and seek her out. But she was nowhere to be found. I looked outside, in the kitchen and living room, but she wasn't there. Maybe she was in the bathroom or in her room freshening up. Eventually, someone told me to check the basement. The stairs to the basement were behind the kitchen, and when I opened the door, the stairs were covered in a blue, ethereal glow. Walking down the stairs was like going underwater, there was no fluorescent light, just the deep blue of Neon LEDs. Her father was a DJ, and he kept all his equipment downstairs. The blue light was from his party rig and past his boxes and his turntables was a seating area; two cream leather couches turned to face each other, and a Lazy Boy that swiveled on its axis on the far side of the room. A few people were down here, a small group huddled on one couch zoned out and staring at the ceiling, high and taking comfort in the blue neon fever dream that painted the white walls of the basement. On the other couch was a couple. She was on top of him. His hands were roaming her back and her thighs and her lips were on his neck and her hands were in his hair. I heard the smack of their lips and their heavy breathing. In the blue light, they looked otherworldly, a Dali come to life, an unintelligible mix of orifices and limbs. But when she turned her head, her eyes went wide. She extricated herself from the boy on the couch, slapping away his hands as he groped for her absent body. It was Morgan. She stood there, frozen, her mouth gesticulating as if trying to churn out syllables and turn them into words, but the harder she tried, the more her lips quivered, and nothing came out. Finally, as I turned to leave, doing my best to keep my poker face intact, she reached out and grabbed my arm.

"Ryan... I..."

The words never came. I stormed up the stairs and into the kitchen, pushing past the couple pressed up against the fridge, ignoring their complaints as Morgan stomped up the stairs behind me. I was already out the door and down the porch steps when she emerged and slammed it closed.

"Ryan, wait up, please don't leave."

I wanted to keep walking but I stopped and turned around to face her. It was dark on her front lawn, the only light coming from the open doorway. She looked small and scared, like a child waking up from a dream only to realize they're caught in a nightmare. She descended the brick steps with her right hand on the rail to steady herself. She was sober, the tipsy, happy girl that leaned into my chest gone. She shuddered as a breeze passed between us. We were a few feet away and, for the first time, I refused to close the gap. She inched forward, drawing closer, testing the waters, watching my face for any sudden movement.

"Will you let me explain?" She asked.

"What's left to say, Morgan?" I retorted, surprised at the venom in my voice.

"His name is Chris. We've been dating for two weeks. I meant to tell you, but I... I don't know... Maybe, I knew that telling you would end this."

"What is this?" I asked.

"I don't know. I don't know, but what I do know is that I don't want to lose you."

I should have said I love you, right there and then. But I was too angry, and I knew I had no right to be. She was single, she didn't owe me any loyalty outside what a platonic friendship demanded. But the months of flirting, cuddling up together, the things we left unsaid on the phone, the way our hearts beat when we touched, the almost-kisses, the time spent in bed debating if we should do what our bodies told us to do, all that had to mean something. Sure, we weren't dating, but we weren't friends.

I took a deep breath. I always forgot how short she was. I was a full foot taller than her. I always laughed when she got mad, she'd do this thing with her lips while play-punching me in the ribs. I'd feign pain, laughing all the way to the floor where she'd get on top of me and start tickling me. We'd collapse next to each other, breathless, and often we'd turn on our sides to face the other, and sometimes, if we were daring, we'd lock our hands and press our foreheads together. More than once our lips almost touched, and there were a few moments when it almost went too far. We'd grab at each other and start pulling on our clothes, but before we were naked, we'd stop and dress and go back to what we were doing before our play fighting almost turned into sex.

"Enjoy your birthday, Morgan. I hope you like your gift. Read the card if you want, but I think it's best if I go."

"Ryan, I'm sorry."

"I know you are."

I had the strong desire to run, to sprint past the endless rows of suburban homes, and lose myself in the meaningless of it all. The same cars, the same lawn gnomes, the same postcard families who spoke in the same Long Island accents, and raised their kids as clones to occupy the same homes until they either went bankrupt or the earth imploded. What was the point of it all, what was the point of love, if only to give it away and lose it all in one breath? In coming to love Morgan, I'd left myself open, and for the first time in a long time, I'd allowed myself to feel. I'd allowed myself to move past the wall of hardened flesh left there by my father, and back out into the world where my heart was left vulnerable to the elements. Either I was undeserving, or the world was set against me, and when you were a teenager and everything felt world-ending, you were prone to rash pronouncements. There, in front of Morgan, heart rendered in two, I vowed to never love again, to retreat behind the callouses my father formed and live my life from the outside looking in, always aware, a voyeur, a watchman looking for the first sign of invasion.

After graduation, my mother offered to send me to Puerto Rico to spend some time with my grandfather. She offered to send me with a friend, but I declined. I wanted to be alone, and for the first time I cared little about the summer I'd miss back home. Everyone prepared to move on, go away to school and start lives of their own. We'd said our goodbyes and by the time graduation came and went, I was ready to leave high school behind.

I landed in Ponce, for the first time by myself. My grandfather had arranged for his friend to pick me up from the airport. He didn't give me a number and I didn't know who to look for, so I milled about in baggage claim looking for someone who might have recognized me. Then again, Abu hadn't seen me in two years. I'd changed, I'd grown out my facial hair and covered my baby face in what was the beginnings of a beard. My hair was cropped short in a military-style buzz cut. I wore ripped denim, a black shirt, and a thin camo army jacket from an army surplus store, with black Doc Martens to boot, a far cry from the baggy shorts and flashy Jordans I used to wear.

After a few minutes of circling the baggage claim, I saw the name Díaz hastily scrawled across am 8x11 sheet of paper. It was held by a man, at least in his sixties, short, rotund, with leathery bronze skin, and a salt and pepper mustache propped on his upper lip like an outcropping of cliff-stone. I walked over to him, doing my best not to acknowledge him until the very last minute, in case he wasn't there for me, and I was forced to explain myself with what very little Spanish I possessed. Díaz was a popular name. He could've been there for anyone, but as I inched closer his eyes widened in recognition.

"Hyan, Hyan!"

He shouted and pointed his finger at me like he was a prospector striking gold. I adjusted my bag on my shoulder and picked up my pace. The pronunciation of my name felt odd yet familiar, and though I knew enough to associate it with me, it always felt as if Hyan was another person. An alter ego, someone I could've been if I had spent my youth in Puerto Rico rather than Queens.

I followed him to his car, an old Buick with chipped black paint and cream-colored leather seats, more yellow than cream now from years sitting open under the hot island sun. We drove in silence. I wanted to ask me how he noticed me but couldn't figure out how to ask him in my broken Spanish, and to be honest, a tall, fair-skinned gringo awkwardly milling about an airport was an obvious giveaway.

It was the midafternoon, and the sun dominated the sky, sending sweat down my back and into all the corners and crevices I was desperate to keep dry. I ripped off my army jacket and lowered the window to cool down the car. The air smelt like salt. The Caribbean Sea followed us as we dipped and dashed between cars, keeping pace as we followed the winding highway from Ponce to Yauco.

My cell phone vibrated in my pocket, and when I looked down at it, I saw a new message alert scrolling across the screen on my Blackberry. It was Morgan. I spent a few minutes staring at the notification, debating whether I should open it or delete it without looking at it. While we hadn't formally ended our friendship, I'd been keeping my distance. Her new boyfriend didn't like when I was around, and eventually, Morgan stopped inviting me out when they were together. We occasionally hung out alone, but I quickly put an end to that too. She treated me like an escape, and I had no desire to be someone's secret rendezvous. I'd ignored her for the past couple of days, only picking up to let her know that I was heading to the island and my service would be spotty. I fingered the screen, running my finger over the message, as if with enough passes I could erase it and put her out of my mind. But curiosity got the better of me. I ducked my head down and allowed my eyes to linger over her name. Morgan, an omen of death, a symbol of peace, red-breasted, flighty, and free. I selected the message and read it under my breath like an incantation, as if reading it would summon her here. Even over text, her voice was distinct, and as I read, I heard it ringing in my ears.

Morgan: "Did you get in okay? Let me know when you land if you can. Have a wonderful trip, maybe next time I could go with you? Think about it. Love ya, Ry." (12:30 pm)

I closed my phone and stuffed it into my bag. Abu's friend turned on the radio, and as we drove, I let the music wash over me. I'd answer later. I lowered the window. The sea air filled the car, and the sound of Morgan's voice grew softer and softer until it was drowned out by the sound of wind and screeching gulls.

I spent most of my time wandering around Yauco. In the morning, I'd wake up and pick up bread from the panderia and bring a loaf back to share with Irma and Abu. Every morning, we'd sit around the kitchen table enjoying coffee and bread while they asked me about college and my plans. I'd chosen to stay local and attend a private catholic university thirty minutes from home. While I reveled at the thought of getting out from under my mother's roof, I loved the city too much to leave it behind. Plus, we couldn't afford room and board, we could barely afford the out-of-pocket expenses for my first semester. After hearing about our money troubles, Abu agreed to help and wired a few thousand dollars to my mother to cover the cost of my freshman year. When I told Abu that I was majoring in history, he started asking me random historical facts and would laugh when I was left stumped and would proceed to proudly announce the correct answer. Abu had gone to college in the states. He didn't finish, but he was a well-read and literate man, and though his house was devoid of books, he often quoted from classics as if he had them memorized.

After breakfast, I went to the courts to shoot around, playing against the locals until my stomach growled and my legs were numb. Then, it was back to the house where Irma whipped me up a plate of rice and beans and whatever meat was left over from the previous night. Sometimes, I skipped lunch and followed my new friends to the beach in the back of an old Ford pickup that jumped a few feet in the air every time it hit a curb. There, I'd enjoy the waves and try my best to make conversation in broken bits of Spanish dominated by English. I even managed to snag a kiss from one of the girls who hung out with us. Her English was good, and she was preparing to go to college in the states. She told me she had a boyfriend, but since I was from the mainland no one would know. We walked down the beach out of the sight of her friends and kissed in the water. It felt more like a transaction than anything else, and when we were done, she winked and walked away and didn't talk to me for the rest of the day. When I saw her in town a few days later, she ignored me and proceeded into a store followed by her boyfriend, and after that day I never saw her again.

It took me a week to text Morgan back. It was short and sweet and accompanied a pixelated picture I snapped with my cell phone. She responded shortly after with a picture of her suntanning in her backyard, wishing she was in PR with me. Her hair hung loosely around her face and sunglasses hid her eyes. I pictured her here with me, sprawled out together on the beach, swimming in the ocean, the water the only thing between us. But I quickly dismissed the image, shut off my phone, and left it on my nightstand. Part of me was elated, she was thinking about me and that had to count for something, but that was quickly eclipsed by anger, anger at myself for letting her get in my head, and anger at her for stringing me along.

I walked outside and leaned against the railing that surrounded my grandfather's house. The tile was cold under my feet and the air was warm. The sun was setting, and the town was quiet save for the clip-clop of horse hooves as two young black boys rode by saddleless on brown mounts, looking like two conquering heroes riding into town to receive their crown. The door creaked behind me, and Abu joined me at the railing. We watched the boys ride by while the sun slipped past the hills that bordered the horizon, turning their green peaks purple and pink.

"¿Sabes como conducir?"

I shot a dumbfounded look at my grandfather, who upon seeing my bewildered expression shook his head and smiled.

"Do you know how to drive?"

"A little, but my parking sucks," I replied.

"Bueno, it's time for you to learn. Venga, follow me."

I followed my grandfather to his car. I stood by the driver's side, unsure of what to do next until Abu thrust his keys into my chest. I got behind the wheel, and Abu with a lot of grunting and cursing slid into the passenger seat beside me. I put the key in the ignition and felt the car rumble to life, coughing and wheezing like it was recovering from a nasty cold. The engine idled and I adjusted my mirrors, fidgeting with the rearview until the driveway appeared behind me. Abu reached past me and pulled the gate key from behind the shade. The gates were open, the car was running, and I was ready. I put the car in reverse and let my foot up off the break. We moved slowly down the driveway. Abu watched me, his eyes flicking back and forth between my hands and the road. I checked my rearview and pulled the car out of the driveway before putting it in drive and giving it a little gas.

I followed my grandfather's directions, turning left, then right, then left again until we were on the main road that cuts through Yauco. The normally brightly colored buildings looked muted and dim in the light of the fading sun, and soon I had to turn the headlights on. Every so often Abu would critique my driving, but after ten minutes, he stopped altogether. The roads were empty, and the town was quiet save for the bars, where rotund men laughed and jeered at the TV screen while slamming down dominoes on a wooden table that looked like it was about to break. After another ten minutes, the town was behind us. Abu motioned for me to turn onto a dirt road. The car bumped and jolted as we drove over the uneven earth. We were going uphill. As we reached the crest of the mound, the ground leveled out and all Yauco stretched before us, looking small and insignificant, a million miles away, what the earth must look like from space, little dots of light against the all-consuming black of cosmic night.

"I used to come here when I was a boy," said Abu. "Sometimes with friends, other times alone. Especially when I was alone."

I looked over at Abu. He stared off into the distance. He never really talked about his childhood, in fact, I barely knew anything about his early years. I forgot that he was once a boy like me, full of dreams and regrets, heartache and loss, unsure of the future, still coming to grips with who he was and who he longed to be.

"Do you have any regrets?" I asked.

The question hung in the air, and I kicked myself for having ruined an intimate moment with such a jarring question. But after a few seconds, Abu sighed.

"Of course, mijo. Too many to count. But my greatest regret was losing your grandmother."

Abu never talked about my grandmother, Noni, as I called her. They were divorced when my mom was about sixteen and neither brought the other up. For the first few years of my life, the fact that they were both my maternal grandparents was lost on me. She lived in New Hampshire, he lived in Puerto Rico, and the last time they'd been in the same room was for my parent's wedding in the eighties. I learned early on not to bring one up to the other. When I first asked Noni about Abu, she brushed me off and rolled her eyes, and when I brought up Noni to Abu, my mom pulled me to the side and explained that we shouldn't talk about Noni around Irma and that I should respect her as Abu's wife. But now, hearing Abu mention Noni, I saw my opportunity to finally figure out what happened between them.

"What happened between you two?" I asked.

Abu laughed.

"It's a long story, but I think we have time. I met your grandmother through my sister. You see, my sister was dating your Noni's brother, Julio, a gaunt and frail fellow with bags under his eyes from late nights playing the clubs, and a somewhat testy relationship with alcohol. He was a salsero, or at least he wanted to be, and he and his band played a small club in Ponce on Friday nights. It was tight and hot, and when it was full we were packed in and herded about like cattle, doing our best to dance and drink without getting swallowed by the swaying crowd. My sister would go and see him play on Fridays and I'd tag along to make sure that she got home okay. I'd stand in the corner and watch the band while my sister danced by the band pit to impress Julio and, when they were fighting, to make him jealous. One night, Julio invited me to grab dinner with him and his band after their set. My sister begged me to go with them, knowing it was the only way I'd let her hang around him and his band after the show. We left the club and ended up at a bar. My sister was sixteen and I was only eighteen, but back then no one cared. We huddled around a table in the back, my sister on Julio's lap, smiling and winking while he talked with his bandmates about another gig in San Juan. That's when I saw her. She was behind the bar with a tray of amber glasses balanced on one hand while she wiped a spill up with another. Her hair was cropped short just under her ears and was a startling orange red, like her head was aflame or crowned in a halo. She was short and thin, and her pale skin shone with a dim glow like the surface of the moon in a clear sky. I went up to the bar, but she paid me no mind, and when she did acknowledge me, it was with a roll of her eyes. I later learned that she was Julio's sister, and that despite her standoffishness, she thought I was guapo, though a little too arrogant for her taste."

Eventually, I got my sister to set up a double date with Julio and his sister Nerida. We went to dinner and drank rum on a beach not too far from town. Julio and Maria ran off and left me and Nerida alone. We bantered back and forth, and she gave as good as she got. But, at the end of the night, when the moon was high and bright, we kissed. I knew then that I wanted to marry her. Sadly, that had to wait. Uncle Sam came calling and I had to do a tour in Korea against the Reds. She said that she'd wait for me and write as often as she could. I spent most of my tour reading her letters, imagining myself back on the island, on that beach beneath the moon."

"Did you guys get married when you got back?" I asked.

Abu shook his head.

"When I got back from tour, I packed up my bags and went stateside. For the first time in my life, I recognized the largeness of the world, and how much lay beyond the small island I called home. I wrote to apologize and promised her I'd return. She didn't write back. I was young and selfish. I spent four years stateside going to school and working. I started to build a life for myself. I settled in Nueva York and lived with some cousins in Brooklyn. I got my realtor license and was soon making decent money flipping homes in Sunset Park. It was then I saw your Noni again. She'd moved with her brother to the Bronx. We bumped into each other at a diner. Her hair was still cropped short, and she wore a defiant look on her face. She refused to talk to me. Eventually, I convinced her to come by my place for coffee. A year later, we were married. Pretty soon your mother came along, and your Noni became a full-time mom. I retreated into my work. We grew apart. She wanted to go to school. She wanted to work, to have something of her own. But I wouldn't have it. Who would take care of Marie, I'd ask. She suggested a sitter. I told her a daughter needed her mother. We fought constantly. I started drinking, and when your mom turned fifteen, Noni packed her bags and took your mom with her."

Abu looked haggard and worn, as if remembering aged him. Here was a man I didn't know. Gone was the ever-smiling grandfather of my youth. Here was an old man burdened with regret, desperate to go back and change the past, trapped in a future of his making. You saw the years he could've had pooled beneath his eyes. Each tear, a portrait of what could've been—an endless deluge of imagined futures. He wiped his face with a handkerchief, wiping away the life he could've had, and turned to face me, his eyes set and narrow, a picture of a man who'd long ago decided to accept his fate.

"Now, mind you, I love Irma. I do. But I still imagine what our lives could've been. Your Noni was special. She was right to leave me, and I've spent most of my life wondering what would've happened if I'd fought for her."

The car rolled to a stop. We were at the end of the road. The car idled as we sat there in silence. I thought about Abu, my grandmother, and Morgan. I imagined myself aged and withered with gray hair and slurred speech, speaking to my grandson about the girl that could've been. I decided to call her. I had no clue what I wanted to say but sitting there with my grandfather behind the wheel of his car, I realized that it would be better to say something than not say anything at all.

To this day, I've never regretted making that call.

Chapter 7:

2011

I can't remember a time when I wasn't in church. My earliest memories are of straight-backed wooden pews and late-night prayer meetings that ran way past midnight and into the first hours of early morning. My parents ate, slept, and breathed church. More often than not, we were there three days out of the week, twice during the week, and all day on Sunday. My childhood consisted of fire and brimstone of sermons, Sunday school lessons, and songs—the inane, repetitious kind designed to annoy parents and keep kids entertained and impart some moral lesson which was usually ignored.

Most of it went over my head. But whatever drew my parents to religion was lost on me. Church was rote, mundane, as a part of my life as brushing my teeth and taking a bath. Religion was my normal and up until the age of twelve, I assumed that everyone else went to church as well. I couldn't fathom a world without a crucifix hanging over my head, so for the most part I paid it no mind. God was like a stain on a rug that never goes explained. It's just there. After a while, you forgot it existed, or at least until company came over and you had to move the sofa a few inches to the left to cover it up.

It wasn't until I was fifteen that I had any real religious experience. Up until then, I believed in God the way kids believe in their parents. I believed enough to obey but not enough to quell the aching doubt that they were wrong about everything. I tortured my Sunday school teachers with what-ifs and whys and badgered my parents about the verses they quoted. I was a curious child, always looking, thirsting after truth like a man desperately searching for a desert oasis. I was a cynic through and through, and while my parents seem to have faith built into their bones, I didn't have a believing bone in my body.

At most, God was a curious intellectual exercise, a fascinating question to explore on the weekend when real life took a pause. It was all I knew, but I had this gnawing sensation that there was more, and the more I dug, the more I doubted. By the time I was fourteen, I'd pretty much written off the idea of God altogether. Apathy and disinterest gave way to rejection, and though I was happy to keep up the veneer and go through the motions alongside my parents, I knew that for me God was dead, a decision I made without the help of Nietchze. But that didn't last long, and like O'Connor's Hazel Motes, I was destined for a divine encounter. I was "Christ-haunted." The proverbial crucifix dangled above me like the angled blade at the end of a guillotine, swaying in the breeze, eyeing the nape of my neck, ready to take the plunge and find its mark, all before I knew my head was locked in stocks.

It was a Tuesday. I was fourteen nearing fifteen, my birthday only a few weeks away. It was already dark, and as I walked to the train the wind whipped up a fury. I stuck my hands into my coat pockets and steeled myself against the wind, fighting to keep myself upright as it roared and picked up speed between the concrete monoliths hovering over the sidewalk. I was underdressed. My jacket was thin. I shivered and sucked my teeth and in an act of defiance lifted my head into the gale. The wind gnawed at my exposed flesh and sent tears streaming down my face. I arrived at the subway station a shivering mess and waited impatiently for the next train to arrive while I tried to warm myself up by jumping up and down in place. Eventually, I heard rumbling. The head of the train emerged from the end of the tunnel like an iron earthworm breaking through the dirt. The car was packed but I was grateful for the body heat. I set my bag down between my legs and leaned against the doors. The train took off and I shifted my weight to compensate for the gentle sway, pretending that I was a sailor at sea getting used to his sea legs.

I was headed to Brooklyn on the F train, a thirty-something-minute ride that took me from Queens through Manhattan and into the heart of Downtown Brooklyn. I was on my way to church. For the past few weeks, I'd managed to excuse myself from these mid-week gatherings, citing schoolwork and basketball practice as the reasons for my absence. But basketball season ended, and my mom grew more and more convinced that a train was a perfectly fine place to get some homework done. I eventually conceded and, to keep the peace at home, I decided to go to church during the week at least once a month. I already went on Sundays, and sometimes I went on Fridays when they did youth nights, though usually, I slipped out with some friends to catch a party nearby or spent the service chatting up one of the girls in attendance. Of course, this didn't matter to my mom. The prayer meeting was different. She was an old-school Pentecostal through and through, and with my dad out of the picture, she figured we needed all the prayer we could get.

The train made me sleepy and, even on my feet, I had to fight to keep my eyes open. That Tuesday I was exhausted and more than once I woke up with a start as I felt my body slump against the woman standing next to me. The stops passed by in a monotonous blur, each station looking the same save for the change in name. I grew more alert as we neared my stop. In New York City, there was nothing worse than missing your stop. A fifteen-minute trip could easily turn into an hour and with the way trains ran, you were considered lucky if your train managed to arrive on time. I managed to wake myself up enough to notice that my stop was next.

The breaks whined as the train slid into the station. The doors slid open with that familiar hiss. I slung my backpack over my shoulder, zipped up my jacket and pressed past the throng of people who stood between me and the door. As I worked my way through the crowd, I noticed how close we all really were. Our bodies were pressed up against each other, shoulder to shoulder, back-to-back, each of us pretending not to notice, trying our best to hold our heads above the rest like we were drowning and desperately fighting for air, each of us close enough to feel each other's skin, separated only by anonymity.

I grew up hearing about the immanence of God, the incarnation, and his proximity to man. But if God was real and as close as they said, he might as well have been a stranger on a subway car, close enough to touch but impossible to know.

It was snowing. Little white specks landed on my face and quickly turned into slush as my hot breath escaped my lips. All around me the snow desperately tried to gain a foothold on the concrete, but the gray pavement gave no ground. They were repulsed as soon as they touched down and coated the streets with a thin and shiny layer of moisture. Overnight, the water would turn into ice, and the morning rush would grind to a halt as passengers carefully made their way across the impromptu rink outside the station's entrance. The church wasn't far. It lay between Smith and Gallatin on the corner of Livingston. I crossed Fulton Avenue and followed the long train of commuters who made their way home. Fulton bustled with activity, and, despite the snow, the vendors were still out peddling fake Louis Vuitton and off-brand fragrances that all seemed to smell the same, like a bouquet of aluminum flowers. I stopped inside a Pizza Hut and scrounged up enough money to buy a Personal Pan Pizza (I was always a sucker for alliteration), which I quickly scarfed down with a long, cold swig of Coca-Cola. I had a few minutes to spare, so I sat by the storefront window and watched the snow obscure the avenue. I checked my watch; the service was about to start. I grabbed my bag and crossed the street and made my way to front of the church building.

    The wooden doors were opened wide. Men and women trickled in, shook the snow off their heads, and proceeded down the corridor to the sanctuary. I followed behind them and shook myself free of snow. It felt off me in droplets. I felt the arm of my jacket. It was wet, and I felt it seeping into my shirt. I removed my jacket and folded it under my arm, ignoring the moisture that spread across my ribs. Thankfully, the church was warm, and as I made my way down the corridor the last of the cold drained from my bones.

    The doors opened to reveal a massive theater. Rows of chairs stretched from the stage to the far corner of the room. A golden cross hung suspended in the air above the podium, dominating the space with its gravitational pull, drawing even unwilling eyes to contemplate the rudimentary sign. The room was dark, but even in the dim lighting you saw the moving throng, men and women from all walks of life milling about in the rows, looking for their seats, talking in hushed whispers with their heads bent low like a murder of crows eyeing a corpse. Some were kneeling, their hands clasped, mouths moving, their elbows digging into their seats, unaware of the cold, hard floor beneath their knees. These were the zealots, the real believers, and unlike their gossiping counterparts, they seemed to take God seriously, brought to their knees before the cross, caught up in God's all-consuming fire. I looked for my mother to no avail. There wasn't enough light to make out the particulars of faces. Eyes, lips, noses, and ears lost their definition. As if their shadows had crawled out from under them to trade places. I found a seat near the back and opened my phone to shoot my mother a quick text. The light from my phone seemed to disturb my neighbors, and as quickly as I could, I sent off a hurried 'here' before shoving my phone into my pocket and apologizing to the older woman sitting next to me. Her face was stern and avian, and she didn't bother to respond. She adjusted her head and fixed her gaze on the two women chatting further down the aisle. If they felt her eyes boring holes into their backs, they didn't seem to care. They carried on, and as the woman next to me narrowed her eyes, I wondered if she would say something. But before she could shush them, the music kicked in. Everyone stood and I stood with them. The old organ shook the room with the first few notes from some chorus I no longer remembered. The people sang along. I think I sang, too, or at the very least hummed and tried to keep up with the wordy verses.

The music died down and a man walked across the stage. He was tall. Too tall. His arms swung beside him like overgrown vines and his head turned on a neck reminiscent of a giraffe or an ostrich, his small skull precariously placed on a rising peak. His face was fleshy, and the bags and crow's feet betrayed his age. He towered over the podium and took his time surveying the crowd. His eyes were gray like storm clouds and when he passed by me, I dropped my chin and avoided his gaze. I knew full well he couldn't see me, but I couldn't be sure. He had wise eyes. The kind of eyes that always saw more than they let on, always peering past the veil and through the fog. I willed my head up, unwilling to be bowed, but when our eyes locked, I ducked and didn't dare look again. I swore, it was like looking into the eyes of God. As the band swelled, his hands gripped the lectern in a white-knuckled grip, and when he bowed his head, the band followed suit. The room was quiet, and though I stood alone, it felt like all their eyes were on me. I shifted back and forth, daring not to lift my head. The man spoke, and as he spoke, my chest pounded. Faster and faster until all I heard was the blood rushing to my head. His voice grew louder. I could barely stand. I sat down and put my head between my legs. My face was wet. Tears pooled on my pant legs. I shuddered and tried to catch my breath, but no matter how hard I tried the tears kept coming. A sob left my lips. He spoke softly now, and I fell to the cold, hard marble and placed my head against the seat in front of me. The wood was cool. I was on fire. Everything fell away. All I felt was the wood and the marble and my heart beating uncontrollably. There was no time. I was adrift in the void. The void was God and, like a ship adrift with no land in sight, I gave up hope and gave into the vast emptiness. Then, suddenly, I was back. My neighbor nudged me. She was trying to get by. I got up. My knees were covered in dust and my forehead stung where it had pressed into the wood. I stood and tried to process what happened. But whatever I felt was gone. I found my mother by the doors. She asked me how it went, and I said nothing. In the passenger seat of her Mazda, I stared out the window and watched the cars pass by. It all seemed so trivial, monotonous. Everyone in their lanes riding along predetermined paths. I was convinced. There had to be more to life than this. I tried to think back to the service, to the words on the pastor's lips, but everything was hazy, and the harder I tried to remember, the more the memory slipped from my grip. I was only fourteen and already burdened with a terrible truth; God was somewhere out there, and he wouldn't rest until found me.

    I spent the next week trying to recapture that feeling.

    I'd wake up before school, drop to my knees, and ramble on and on until all that was left was an awkward silence and red blotches where the rug burned my knees. When that didn't work, I took a crack at fasting and went days without eating in hopes to force myself into a transcendental state. I spent hours on the internet and in the library rummaging through the Desert Fathers, The Life of Saint Francis, and Theresa of Avila's Interior Castle. I understood almost nothing of what I read, and the parts I did understand required a pseudo-masochism I wasn't ready for. I was enamored by the mystics and in my pursuit of God, I discovered that any religion worth its salt is worth dying over, not in some holy jihad, or in a tub of Kool Aid, but in a religion that required all of you. If God was indeed all-powerful and all-consuming, then certainly he'd require nothing less than all of me. The thought haunted my dreams, and when I went to bed, all I saw was fire, holy fire, and God's hand outstretched, reaching toward me, an inevitability I couldn't avoid.

Eventually, my fervor faded. Nothing seemed to work. The tears wouldn't come and no matter what I did, that overwhelming feeling of the transcendence didn't return. I knew that God was out there, but in my fifteen-year-old opinion, he was fickle at best, and if he wanted me, he knew exactly where to find me. Over the course of a winter, I'd gone from atheist to true believer to agnostic all in a month's time, and like most fifteen-year-olds, my attention shifted as quickly as it focused. Pretty soon my existential crisis retreated to the back of my subconscious to join the other life-altering questions we all tend to put off until we're too old to look for answers and too lazy to change.

    But it wasn't long until God began to rear his bearded head. In the fall of 2011, I started my second year of college at a Catholic University in Queens, not far from the apartment I shared with my mom. That fall I was enrolled by my adviser in a theology course, one of three every student is mandated to take. The class was called the Mystery of God, and my professor was a priest and a member of the Vincentian order that founded the school. He was a rotund, elderly man by the name of Father Kristoff. Every day he walked into class with his Roman collar barely visible beneath the jowl that swayed back and forth from his hair-speckled chin like a pendulum possessed by some otherworldly power. Unlike him, his lectures were thin and concise. We spent most of our time talking through the readings, debating and discussing freely while he sat back and observed, offering clarification only when necessary and chastisement when our thinking was uncritical and our questions too simple.

I couldn't get enough.

We read Aquinas's Summa, the poetry of Saint John of the Cross, and wrestled with the mind-bending work of Origen, Athanasius, Augustine, and the like. All the big questions I ignored were dragged kicking and screaming to the forefront of my mind. Something clicked. These were the questions that mattered, and I finally had the opportunity to explore them with other like-minded souls. We banded together and continued our debates on the Great Lawn, and in-between classes during Father Kristoff's office hours.

I never shared what I experienced as a teen. In many ways, I was embarrassed by the experience. For most of my peers, God was an intellectual exercise, a psychological phenomenon useful only to explore the inner workings of the human psyche. To bring up my own experience would be to cross the imaginary boundary between academic exploration and religious zeal. Personal experience was for fanatics and fundamentalists. I played along as long as I could. In the beginning, it was fun. I enjoyed the intellectual rigor of our academic debates. But that only lasted for so long. I grew tired of talking about the idea of God. Unlike my peers, I wanted to go beyond the theoretical. I wanted to go where our academic experience couldn't, into the very mystery of God himself.

It was a Monday. The Great Lawn was covered in a wet blanket of fog. The sun was barely up. Everything was obscure and gray. The University was silent. I was alone. As I crossed the lawn, I felt the dewy grass squelch under my feet. On the other side of the lawn, a light shimmered in the fog. It was the open door of the chapel. The light streamed out and beat back the fog as if it guarded the entrance against the darkness. I went inside and sat down. The room was round. An altar made of black granite sat in the middle of the room. I felt its weight, its gravity, and like a black hole, it pulled me in. The round room acted like the altar's event horizon, once it was crossed there was no escape. A bell rang and the service began. Father Kristoff walked down the center of the circle. He stood behind the altar. It was just us and a professor I knew from the history department. The service passed by in a blur. But then, we came to the consecration.

I watched Kristoff lift the host. His eyes never left the wafer. I saw it in his eyes. He had it, the look I so desperately desired. The look of someone lost in the total otherness of God. I watched him closely. His face, his eyes, his hands. All taught with pent-up kinetic energy. He looked ready to explode, like he was seconds away from spontaneous combustion. I imagined him there, on fire, still holding the host, his skin gray with ash, a smile on his face, his voice barely audible, whispering, "God's an all-consuming fire."

The service was over. I grabbed my bag and made my way outside. The sun was up, and the fog was gone. I moved away from the chapel entrance and fought with my lighter to get a cigarette lit. It refused to light. I looked through the translucent neon plastic and saw that the lighter was out of fuel. I tossed the empty lighter back into my bag. I had class in an hour, and I hoped to catch Kristoff after chapel. I turned around as he emerged. He stopped and, much to my surprise, he grabbed a pack of cigarettes from his jacket pocket. He gave me a curt wave and I took that as an invitation to join him

"Can I bother you for a light?" I asked. Father Kristoff reached into his jacket pocket and pulled out a silver Zippo. The bronze casing was faded. A green patina crept up the sides like an overgrowth of vines, snaking this way and that up the hinge and over the sides. I gripped the flint with my thumb and pushed it down and away. The yellow flame twisted and turned in the wind. I lowered my cigarette and drew until the end was smoldering with orange embers. I took a long, deep draw.

"I notice you didn't come up for the mass," said Father Kristoff.

"I'm a Protestant," I replied.

"Yet you came to a Catholic Mass."

The campus was waking up now. Students armed with cups of coffee were on their way to class. The sun beat down on the lawn, no longer hidden behind the horizon, but on display for all to see. I lifted my head to savor the warm rays washing over my face. I looked over at Father Kristoff. He'd finished his cigarette. I knew if I waited any longer, I'd miss my chance, and so before he turned around to head off to his office, I offered to walk with him. I told him about my experience as a young teen. He listened; his eyes fixed in front of him, never turning to face me. When I finished, he paused. We stood there on the path between the library and the liberal arts college. He had one arm tucked under the other, his chin resting in his hand. He looked up, a thin smile forming along the curve of his lips.

"Look around you, Ryan. What do you see?"

"People, the lawn, the library, you."

"Where is God? He's not as far as you think. You're not going to find him in the whirlwind, or in the fire, or in some ecstatic vision. God's way too subtle for that. The world's a looking glass. Turn your head at the right angle and you'll see more than you bargained for."

"God's here. Not in some grand vision, but in the everyday and the ordinary, the mundane, the bread and wine, the people walking by. 'One that looks on glass, on it may stay their eye; or if they pleaseth, through it pass, and then the heaven espy.' You see, that's the key. God shows up where we least expect him, and if you go looking for him in some extraordinary experience, you probably won't find him. But if you learn to see, truly see, to look again at the world with wonder, you'll discover that God is truly all in all. But you have to be humble enough to see. I'm not discounting your experience, those moments happen, but even for saints, visions are few and far between. The point of a vision is to move beyond it. To see the world in light of it."

At the end of the semester, I booked a trip to Puerto Rico. When my grandfather first arrived on the island, he used some of his money to help start a little church in the neighboring town of Guayanilla. The church was celebrating an anniversary and planned to honor Abu for his contributions to the community. After hearing how much my presence would mean to him, I promised to fly down once finals were over.

On the last day of class, I handed in my essay to Father Kristoff. In it, I expounded on the sacramental theology of the Roman Catholic Church, focusing on Aquinas's synthesis of Christian theology and Aristotelian metaphysics, particularly his understanding of communion, and transubstantiation: how seemingly ordinary bread and wine become the body and blood of Christ. According to Aristotle, the substance of a thing was consistent with its accidents. But Aquinas made the shocking claim that while the bread and wine retain their accidents, their substance was radically transformed. The host looked, and smelled, and felt, and tasted as it should, but the host was Christ himself, embodied but hidden. Kristoff gave me an A.

With my papers in and finals done, I took a cab down to JFK to catch my flight to Puerto Rico. My mom was working. I was on my own. I spent the flight combing through a battered copy of *The Complete Poems of*

Gerard Manley Hopkins. I bought it at a second-hand bookstore in the city. I knew he was Catholic and had heard him mentioned once or twice in Kristoff's lectures. The book itself was falling apart. The cover was wrinkled, the pages were yellow, and a few of them dangled helplessly from the book's spine, holding on for dear life every time I flipped through.

I was fascinated by Hopkins's love of nature, and his ability to capture the beauty of things in short, punchy, powerful lines. He saw things I didn't. For Hopkins, the world was alive, something bubbled under the surface of things, and with a few sprung lines, Hopkins could pierce the outer layer, pull back the curtain, and reveal the beauty hidden beneath the surface of ordinary things. For Hopkins, "the world was charged with the grandeur of God." Every nook and cranny of the world teemed with the all too tangible reality of the divine. Every dappled, speckled, and spotted thing. Every creature, every landscape, all of it contained a brief glimpse of glory. Hopkins could see it, Father Kristoff could see it, and as I stared out the window, 30,000 feet in the air, I saw nothing.

I landed in Ponce the day before Abu's celebration. The house was busier than usual. Irma hovered over the stove like a general reviewing troop movements on a map. A few of the women fussed over the dining room table while arguing in Spanish and pointing at the place settings. From what I gathered, they debated where to place the salad forks. I gave them a wave as I dragged my bag into my room. They stopped their arguing to say hi, but as soon as I dropped my hand, they were at it again, a flurry of verbal darts, only some of which I understood and almost all of it something you didn't say in front of company.

The room was the same. The fan still creaked. The pillows were still covered in feathery linen lace, and butterflies still dotted every nook and cranny of the room. Every inch of the house reminded me of how much time had passed. The immovability of the decor highlighted how much I'd changed. I was no longer the little kid running around the house with eyes wide, taking everything in, overwhelmed by the newness of it all. I was older now, weary, and "wise," burdened with the knowledge that time was slipping away and that soon I'd be out in the wider world with the rest of my life ahead of me.

"Getting settled?"

I turned and saw Abu standing in the doorway, resting both of his hands on a silver cane. He wore a brown bowling shirt with thick white stripes that ran up and down the sides of the shirt. In his pocket was a thick, black pocket protector which contained his wire-rimmed reading glasses and a few pens. He stooped over his cane, back bent on a permanent slope. The bags under his eyes made his face look puffy but, despite this, his eyes were as bright as ever. Everything in me wanted to run up and hug him. Instead, I walked up to him and stretched out my hand. He grabbed it and smiled before reaching up to rub the thick layer of hair that now covered the lower half of my face.

"You should shave, you know, no one will give you a job with that hanging from your face."

"I'm in college, Abu, I think I can risk a beard. Plus, the girls seem to like it."

Abu shook his head.

"Aye, nene, you'll waste your mind chasing girls. Shave the beard and go to class. Trust me, girls prefer a man with a degree."

"That didn't stop you."

Abu snorted, grabbed my beard with his hand and gave it a playful tug before walking back out into the hallway.

I went to the bathroom and looked in the mirror. My beard was a bit unruly. I opened the cabinet beneath the sink and searched around for clippers. I found the leather black bag stashed behind some hairspray and a few unused bottles of bright red hair dye Irma used to hide her grays. I opened the bag, plugged in the clipper and slid the guard onto the blade. I watched with a pained expression on my face as my hair collected at the bottom of the sink. I thought about Abu and the look of pride in his eyes when he introduced me to his friends from church. With a sigh, I removed the guard from the blade and shaved my beard until all that was left was a thin layer of five o'clock shadow coloring my pale skin.

When I got out of the bathroom, Abu was in the hallway trying to hide a smile.

"What do you think?" I asked.

He paused, looking me up and down, examining my face, turning it this way and that with his hand.

"So?" I asked again.

"Hmm, I hate to say this, nene, but you looked better with a beard."

Around eight PM, people trickled into the house in groups of three and four. First came the senoras, the matriarchs of the church, many of them widowed, some more recently than others. They were the backbone of the church. Every gathering relied on the food they cooked and the homes they opened. They were at every funeral, wedding, baptism, and graduation. Almost everyone called them titi or tia. They were moms, grandmothers, sisters, and mentors. They always treated me like one of their own. Whenever they stopped by the house while I was visiting, they'd shower me with kisses and gifts. As soon as they walked in, they put down their bags and got to work. The kitchen was crowded but no one seemed to get in anyone's way. They moved like a well-oiled machine, each one balancing a million different things without batting an eye. By eight-thirty, a few more people arrived: a few families with young kids and a young couple who looked like they were about my age.

At nine, the party was in full swing. Abu sat in the corner while people buzzed about him like bees hovering over a flowerbed. Abu wasn't a fan of parties. It was a trait we'd grown to share. Something about the sound of twenty different conversations drove both of us crazy. The only recourse was to find a quiet corner and hunker down. I watched Abu from across the room. For the most part, he was silent. He followed the party with his eyes, smiling at jokes he barely heard while nodding his head at the small snippets of conversation that drifted his way. I stepped away to fill my empty cup with soda, and when I returned, Abu was missing. I asked a few people if they saw where he went and followed the trail of hints outside to the porch.

Abu leaned against the railing with his cell phone to his ear. His eyes were grave. He nodded his head and said something I couldn't hear. He hung up the phone and hung his head.

"Everything okay?" I asked.

He shook his head.

"A good friend of mine is sick. Has been for a while. His family called and said that he's near the end."

"I'm sorry, Abu. Is there anything I can do?"

"Get my keys. I want to be with the family."

"But what about the party?" I replied.

"This is more important. Now quickly, grab my keys, tell Irma where we're going. The church can stay as long as they like."

I ran into the house and pulled Irma to the side to relay Abu's message. She nodded and brought me his car keys. By the time I was outside, Abu was already in the passenger seat ready to go.

The highway was empty. Abu didn't speak much during the ride. He only spoke up to give me directions before going silent again. His eyes were fixed on the road in front of us, as if he tried to will the car forward. I drove as fast as I could, but the old car would only give us so much. When we got off the highway, we took a narrow dirt road into the hill country. The road ran down into a valley and back up along the side of a mountain. Abu's friend lived somewhere up here, in one of those homes that hung off the mountainside, an impossible feat of engineering that stayed standing despite the heavy rains and high winds prone to strike the island during hurricane season. I gently nudged the gas as we wound our way further up the mountain. I took each turn with gritted teeth. My hands started to hurt. I leaned into the wheel, moving my head as close to the windshield as possible, as if arching my body forward would allow me to penetrate the black border beyond the limits of the old car's fading high beams. I knew it wouldn't work but I found the position comforting. It gave me the illusion of control and the confidence to take the narrow turns when they came. As we drew closer, I slowed the car down. Abu stuck his head out of the passenger-side window to make sure we pulled up to the right house. In the dark, they all seemed the same. Moonlight bounced off the tin roofs and bathed the mountainside in silver light. We passed row after row of homes impossibly balanced on wooden stilts. They looked as if they waved in the night, dancing wildly on the edge of oblivion, while our headlights buffeted them like waves, ready to send them careening over the mountain and into the black valley below.

 Abu signaled for me to stop the car. I pulled the car into a narrow driveway. It was barely a driveway at all, a thin patch of dirt tossed up against the side of the house between a thicket of trees and brush. I cut the engine. The lights went out. I couldn't see my hands in front of me. My grandfather reached into the glove compartment and pulled out a flashlight and rapped it against his hand to get it to work. The light stuttered and bloomed. We got out and made our way to the house with only the flashlight to guide our steps. I stood close to Abu, ready to catch him should he stumble in the dark. But his steps were steady. His feet never wavered. He marched up to the door like a soldier in lockstep and knocked twice before stepping away.

 There was a commotion on the other side of the door, bodies moving, feet shuffling, the clattering of plates, and the closing of cupboards. After a few moments, the house went silent. The door swung open revealing a woman in her later fifties. Her face was haggard. Exhaustion was etched into every line of her face, intricate patterns of insomnia permanently carved into her skin like tribal markings, betraying the sleepless nights she was forced to endure. She wore a rumpled nightgown covered in pink flowers, something you'd never wear in front of company unless you were elderly or in dire straits, and given the wrinkles and stains, it was certainly the latter.

As soon as she saw my grandfather, her sad eyes brightened, but only for a moment. Without saying anything, she threw herself at him and collapsed in his arms. Despite his age, he was able to hold her, and for a moment, I saw the Abu I knew as a child, strong, resolute, as dependable as the sunrise, and as steady as a mountain. They whispered in low tones, Abu mostly listening, nodding his head, eyes brimming with water. She turned to me and sized me up and down the way old Puerto Ricans do when they're introduced to a grandchild they've heard so much about. She said something to me in Spanish. All I could do was nod my head and look over at Abu for clarity.

"She says you're a good grandson."

I thanked her and apologized for my poor Spanish. She smiled. Though you could tell smiling strained her, as if those muscles were underdeveloped, atrophied by sadness, used now only rarely, and even then, never moving past her lips.

She led us inside and closed the door behind us. The house was small, everything, the kitchen, the living room, and the dining area was compressed into a small living space not much bigger than most studies in the city. Besides the main door, there were two doors at the back of the room, a bedroom, and a bathroom, and that was it. The floor was covered in linoleum. It peeled in places, curling up from the floor in little white waves, giving the impression that at any moment the whole thing would fold upward and swallow whoever happened to be in the room. We gathered around the kitchen table while Abu's friend, whose name I learned was Mariela, set out two coffee cups in front of us. She and Abu continued to talk in rapid Spanish, and though I tried to keep up, I eventually gave up and turned my attention to our surroundings.

The largest piece of furniture in the room was a wooden bureau covered in picture frames. Black and white photos hung suspended in silver and gold frames. Some were in color, but none looked recent. There, for all to see, was a life laid bare. It was strangely intimate. As if I'd somehow stepped into the private memoirs of a stranger, moments meant to be locked away, now free for me to peruse and explore, an invasion of privacy for sure.

I stared at those faces trapped forever on those thin sheets of photo paper and imagined what it would be like to be frozen in time, unable to move forward or back, stuck in one moment, endlessly repeating the same day, all life reduced to the sound of a broken record, one phrase repeated ad nauseam till judgment day. Change was a luxury we often ignored. We all assumed that life would be full of new things, especially when we were young. We couldn't imagine a life lived on repeat, one day indiscernible from another. But this was Mariela's life. Every day waking up to care for a man who'd never get out of bed, cooking, cleaning, washing, repeatedly, the days of the week adding up to one long, unending day. Her husband had been sick for a while, and for years she'd overseen his care. Day in and day out, she repeated the same, ordinary acts of love and served a man who was in no position to thank her. The pictures were a reminder of the life she'd before his sickness, and ironically a reminder that, like the people in her pictures, she could never leave this scene. But all that was about to change. Her husband was dying.

She poured coffee into our mugs and added a hefty scoop of sugar and some boiled milk. The black color of the coffee relented and lightened as the milk swirled and set, leaving behind a sickly, sweet, golden color. Mariela and Abu continued to chat while I nursed my coffee and waited for it to cool. After blowing on it a few times, I raised it to my lips and took a sip. It was still hot, but not hot enough to burn my tongue.

About halfway through his coffee, Abu got up and went to the room where Mariela's husband slept. He came back out fifteen minutes later and sat back down. At this, Mariela got up and went back into the room.

She left the door open, and I watched her as she stood above her husband, examining his face, trying her best to sear his image into her brain. She bent over, lifted a bowl of water and placed it on the table beside the bed. She took a rag from beside the bowl and gently dipped it until it was soaked. She twisted out the excess water before gently dabbing her husband's forehead and face. The image was biblical, like Jesus washing disciples' feet, a self-giving act, an utter erasure of self. In the face of his pain her needs retreated, the tears she wanted to cry, the God she wanted to curse, all of that was subsumed in this simple act of service. Here, in the privacy of their home, she daily laid down her life for a man who was unable to give her anything in return. There was no mutuality. Only service. Only self-giving. Only love. As she wiped his forehead and pushed back his sweat-matted hair, I realized that God was here. He was hidden, but he was undeniable. He was hidden in Mariella's abnegation, her complete and total denial of self. But he was also hidden by Mariella's husband, a sick man who could only receive an image of grace, utterly dependent and unable to pay back the giver. Here was God, elusive but present, disguised as the sacrificial love of a wife and wrapped up in the brokenness of a dying human body.

I stepped outside. The world was quiet and in the dark. With no one looking, I wept.

Chapter 8:

2013

"Walk it off."

That was my father's advice after I fell off my bike and scraped my knee. I was only five, but I still remember the pain—the bright red valleys cutting across my knee and the black bits of asphalt digging into my skin. I remember falling and screaming out, holding my knee to my chest, staring in horror as the blood ran down my leg. The pain was blinding. My scream was something primal, emerging from our prelinguistic past, in the days before words when the only suitable sound for pain was a gut-wrenching, full-throated roar.

I blubbered and moaned, rocking back and forth on the sidewalk until my dad lifted me to my feet. I was dead weight in his arms and as he lifted me, I went slack, but he wasn't having it. He forced me to stand, and I winced in pain when I tried to put weight on my leg.

"Walk it off," he said.

With snot bubbling above my upper lip and my fists clenched white, I hobbled forward. After a while, my knee went numb. The shooting pain became a dull throbbing, and after a lap around the yard, all I felt was pressure, and after an hour I forgot the pain all together.

As far as I can remember, this was my earliest lesson in coping with pain. I can't blame my father, really. He passed on what he knew, what he learned from his father and his grandfather before him. Ingrained in the male psyche is the need to cover up pain, to squash, swallow, reduce, and ignore any perceived signs of weakness. From a sociological and evolutionary standpoint, this desire makes sense. In male-dominated cultures, where men served as hunters, leaders, and warriors, pain signaled weakness. Weakness hinted at vulnerability, and vulnerability often signaled that a regime change was needed. Entire cultures developed around the idea that strength might make for better men. Spartan warrior culture, Viking coming of age rituals, British stoicism, and Latin Machismo all descend from the incessant need to hide our inner life behind impenetrable walls of emotional armor. My father taught me what all fathers teach their sons—hide your pain, walk it off, steady your gaze, and learn to fight back.

I've been walking it off ever since.

There's a price to repression. The Spartans died out, my dad's father was a drunk, and I was an emotionally stunted college student with low-grade depression and a nasty smoking habit. When I got a call from my mother telling me that Abu was terminally ill with stage four prostate cancer, I wasn't shocked. Like his father and his father before him, he believed that all illness was weakness, and that cancer was something to be hid and suffered in silence until death did its dirty deed.

I found out about his diagnosis on a Saturday. It was winter break; finals were behind me, and I was ready for the holidays. On this Saturday, I was out to lunch with my then-girlfriend, Jacqueline.

We'd met on campus at a club mixer. She was a year younger than me, a sophomore pursuing a degree in a subject I've long since forgotten. She was short, with long, curly ombre locks that ran down her back like rich brown silt littered with gold. She had deep brown eyes, so dark that they looked black, like an abyss devoid of light, all-consuming, twin black holes that drew you in and refused to let you go.

At first, it was purely physical. We both weren't looking for relationships and at our first meeting, we kissed more than we talked.

It was late. We met after class let out and decided to walk the grounds together. We found a bench, and before we knew it, our lips were pressed together as patted and pawed at each other like desperate teenagers on a subway car. After that, we sort of fell into a relationship. Without speaking about it, we talked like we were dating and then, without realizing it, we dated. Pretty soon after that, we were a picture-perfect couple. She introduced me to her friends, and I introduced her to mine. We took each other out on extravagant dates and sometimes, when we felt bold, we'd talk about a future together beyond college. We thought we were in love and at the time, it felt real. But looking back, I realize we had almost nothing in common. Sure, she was beautiful and physically it worked, but beyond that there was nothing else keeping us together. She was a sorority girl, the kind that loved to party, and always wanted to be out. I was an introvert, a history major toying with the idea of being a writer. I liked quiet bars, and whiskey, and preferred the company of the pseudo-intellectuals that occupied my department. I was religious while she wasn't, and we often argued about my religious proclivities, especially my desire to go back to church. We were opposites in every sense of the word and yet, despite this, we were drawn together by an unexplainable magnetism, the all-consuming desire to be each other's all. Like a set of parasites, we burrowed into each other's lives in search of some meaning we couldn't find within ourselves.

Halfway through lunch my cell phone rang. I ignored it. Jacqueline was talking. She was pledging a new line, whatever that meant, and while I chewed on a half-eaten burger she went on about her experience as a pledge. I told her it sounded cultish, but she rolled her eyes.
"It helps the girls bond."
"Can't they bond without the humiliation?"
She sighed and fixed her eyes on the fry she held in her hand. She hated it when I pestered her about Greek Life. I took every chance to tease her about her involvement. I found the whole idea asinine and whenever she brought it up, I made my feelings known. I knew it hurt her, but I persisted, and she hated me for it.
We sat there in silence, awkwardly picking at our food. Moments like this reminded us how different we were, how little we truly had in common. We both thought it, this wasn't working, but neither of us had the courage to say it.
The phone rang again, and I slipped it from my pocket to check who was calling. As soon as I did that, Jacqueline got up from her seat. She had that look on, the one she got when she was annoyed. When we were together, she wanted me totally focused on her. Her need for attention was all-consuming, anything less was a betrayal. I usually conceded to her demands, but this time it bothered me. I ignored her silent protest and picked up the phone.
"Hey, mom, what's up?"
The line was silent. I looked down at my phone to make sure it was working. Sure enough, the call was fine. But when I raised the phone to my ear the line was still dead.
"Mom, are you there? Is everything okay?"
I heard what sounded like sniffling. A sob, drawn-out and long, like a wounded animal caught in a trap slowly bleeding on the forest floor. I

couldn't speak. There were no words for such pain. At that moment, all I could offer my mother was my stunned silence. I waited. Jacqueline stared at me from across the table, the black void of her eyes saying, "see me", but I looked past her, looking for a point of reference to calm my nerves. The TV was on behind her, showing highlights from the game. I watched the scrolling text beneath the talking heads. The words melted into gibberish, until they looked something like hieroglyphics. Everything went blurry, and all I saw was the vague impression of movement on the screen. When my mom started talking, I barely listened. Her voice was garbled and confused; her words kept getting caught in her throat. It took her ten minutes to say anything intelligible. But then the words rolled out of her mouth like thunder:

Abu was dying.

I put the phone down. The world came back into focus. Jacqueline was there, curious and annoyed. I loved her. At least I thought I did. I met her eyes with mine. I felt her gravity, her pull, her push. I was in her orbit now. I let myself go and she drew me in. I was hers and she was mine.

Abu was dying.

I pushed my mother's words to the back of my mind. I looked at Jacqueline, imagining her under me, naked. But the image quickly faded.

Abu was dying.

I got up from our table and took her hand. We paid the bill. When she asked who it was, I said it was nothing.

We went back to her house. Her mother was out, and I laid her down on her bed and lost myself in her.

It was night. We were naked in bed. She ran her hand along my chest and kissed my neck. The phone rang. I got up from her bed and declined the call. She got up and hugged me from behind.

"Is everything okay?"

I kissed her again, put on my clothes, and opened her door. I looked back at her, naked, wrapped in white sheets, golden hair spilling down her back like sunlight, and matter-of-factly, as if I was ordering food over the phone, I said it aloud for the first time.

"Abu is dying."

It was a statement of fact, nothing else. I didn't cry, I didn't move. I stood there saying it over and over again, frozen in place, afraid to move forward, as if staying still would prevent the inevitable.

The phone rang again.

Abu was dying.

We took the next flight out of JFK.

Christmas was only a week away, but when we landed in San Juan, I forgot all about the holidays. The air was oppressive. A hot pool of mist hung in the air coating every inch of us in layers of humid heat. By the time I picked up the rental from the little lot behind the airport, I was covered in sopping sweat. Who could celebrate Christmas here, I thought. I associated Christmas with hot chocolate, blizzards, and ugly sweaters. Here the decor was out of place, Santa looked like he was suffocating, hanging in the window of the rental office with rosy cheeks, less a sign of Christmas spirit and more a sign of heat exhaustion.

I loaded Jacqueline's bag into the trunk and placed it next to mine. Hers, a monogram Louis Vuitton, mine, an old canvas army bag I stole from my dad. I closed the trunk and got in the driver's seat. Jacqueline turned up the AC and we sat there while the cool air washed over us and washed the heat away. I realized that we hadn't spoken since we left her house for the airport. Everything was a blur. By the time I ordered tickets for us, my mom was already on her way to the airport. Once we bought our tickets, we ran to my house to grab my bag. We were off to the airport in the back of a cab. I moved through security like a robot and when we sat down on the plane, I put on my headphones. Jacqueline grabbed my arm and cuddled up next to me. She looked like she wanted to talk, but every time I looked into her imploring eyes, my mouth stayed shut.

I looked over at her. She fixed her makeup in the mirror. It dawned on me. She was going to meet my family. When she finished lining her lips with lipstick, she looked over at me.

"How do I look?" She asked.

I smiled. She looked beautiful. For a moment, I forgot why we were here. I imagined ourselves on vacation, celebrating life and love, heading to a small, beach-side villa where all we would do was drink, sleep, and wash in the waves. I still thought I loved her, and when she looked like this it was hard to deny my attraction, even with my unacknowledged doubts about us. We were still in college. Too young to think about anything beyond graduation. But when she looked at me like that, with her hair framing her tanned face like a saint's halo, and her eyes brimming with unbridled passion, I couldn't imagine a future with anyone else.

"You look wonderful," I replied.

"He speaks. You're lucky I'm used to your brooding, or I might start thinking that you don't want me here."

"I want you here, I do."

My voice trailed off. Reality set in. She reached over and grabbed my hand. I looked at our fingers, intertwined, her grip tight reassuring, my hand loose, barely holding on. We sat there like that for some time. The car was freezing. Jacqueline grabbed her hoodie and put it over her head. I lowered the air. The moment was over. All that was left was for me to put the car in drive. I grabbed the gear stick and felt the familiar thump as the stick clicked into place. Jacqueline put on her shades. I followed suit and, with nothing else keeping us there, I took my foot off the brake and pulled out of the parking lot.

We took the highway from San Juan towards Ponce and cut across the island headed south. Jacqueline was Dominican and she'd never been to Puerto Rico. As we drove, she commented on the similarities and differences between the two islands. As a child, she often spent whole summers in the Dominican Republic, gallivanting about the campo with her cousins under the watchful eye of her grandmother. When she talked about DR, there was a twinkle in her eye and a longing in her voice. The island was an extension of herself, a motherland in every sense of the word, shaping who she was, and giving her a sense of collective identity to which she belonged. DR was her inheritance, her refuge, a place where she was known, and loved. Its people, its sights and sounds, formed an important piece of who she was. I didn't think of PR that way. My relationship was fundamentally different. My associations with the island were distant and disconnected. I was an outsider, an observer, unable to speak the language, and as a result unable to connect with the people who lived here. Sure, I'd made friends as a kid, but I was always at a distance, one step removed, tolerated because I was from New York, an oddity to be questioned and ruefully observed.

Jacqueline turned on the radio and rolled down the windows. She sang along and laughed while she undid her hair and left it to wildly whip around in the wind. The sun was high in the sky. Everything was bright. Her skin was golden, and the gold necklace she wore around her neck shined with stolen light. I didn't know the words, but I tried to sing along anyway. What was the use in being dour in a car for two hours? Maybe it was possible to redeem this trip, I thought. Abu was sick. He was dying. But obsessing over the end would get us nowhere. The holidays were coming, we were in PR, maybe we should make the most of it. Better that than obsess over the inevitability of death. A part of me knew I was deflecting. I'd done enough of it to notice the signs. I didn't care. I'd grapple with reality later. Until then, I might as well enjoy the ride.

When we made the final turn onto my grandfather's street, Jacqueline panicked. She fussed over her hair and was embarrassed by what she wore: ripped, light-wash denim jean shorts and a cropped, hooded sweatshirt that sat above her midriff. She told me that she wanted to change but I insisted she looked fine. Of course, I wasn't the one meeting my partner's family. But, then again, why wear a disguise? This was how she dressed. To become a completely different person to please others was tantamount to the worst kind of betrayal, the betrayal of self, a sin fit for the lowest pits of hell. I said as much but she wasn't buying it. I pulled the car over to a secluded spot beneath some palms. While I kept watch, she grabbed her bag from the trunk and proceeded to change in the passenger seat beside me, stripping off her shorts with difficulty, wiggling this way and that until they were down her thighs and around her ankles. Luckily, the street was empty. She pulled a pair of jeans from her bag and did the same thing in reverse, fighting to get them around her legs and over her ass, her feet on the dash as she stretched and pulled and finally got them around her waist.

"You're going to be hot," I said.

"I thought I was already hot."

She winked, we laughed, and I pulled the car around to the front of Abu's house. I grabbed our bags from the trunk and the gates opened to greet us, this time sans Abu. My mother stood in the driveway. She looked as if she hadn't slept. Her shirt was stained, and her eyes were red and puffy. She didn't even look at Jacqueline. She walked up to me and wept. I held her there, her tears soaking through my shirt. I tried to get her to talk, to get a word from her, but she couldn't speak. Her father was dying. The one dependable man in her life had finally betrayed her, leaving her alone to deal with her wayward husband and her distant son. Irma emerged from the house behind us. She was far more put together. Her hair was done, her clothes clean, and the redness of her eyes was hidden behind globs of mascara and eyeliner.

My mom stiffened as she approached. They'd most likely been fighting. Irma hated to be treated like the other woman, and my mom often overstepped where her father was concerned. Now that Abu was sick, they were at war over his care, and if he passed, they'd be at war over the funeral.

My mom broke away from me and finally introduced herself to Jacqueline. Irma looked her up and down.

"¿Tú hablas español?"

Jacqueline responded in perfect Spanish. Irma looked over at me and nodded in approval.

"Good. Maybe you'll finally learn something."

I took Irma's chiding in stride. We were never close. I had Nonny, Abu's ex-wife, and Irma had her grandson, AJ, her oldest daughter's son from a previous marriage. In some ways she loved us. But as I grew older, I realized that most of the time she tolerated us.

I brought our bags into the house. The house was dark. The blinds were closed. The door to Abu's room was shut. I stood outside it but didn't go in. I couldn't. What do you say to a dying man? Irma saw me by the door. He was sleeping, she said. I sighed with relief.

I had once felt at home here but now I felt like a stranger. Tip-toeing across the tile floor, whispering in the kitchen, unable to joke or crack a smile. Everyone was quiet. My mother wouldn't stop crying. Irma was cold, and poor Jacqueline did her best to bridge the gap between us. She was new. She had no stake in this aside from me. She offered to cook, clean, and take Irma out for errands. But no one ever took her up on the offer. Everyone was in their own world, me included.

Abu slept a lot, something to do with the pain medication. I saw him once or twice in those first few days. He was in bed, his head sticking out from a mound of pillows. He looked like an infant, wrapped and swaddled and immobile. His face was hollow, his cheeks sharp and pronounced, his eyes black and dead, barely acknowledging you when you stepped into the room. I tried to sit by him, but I didn't know what to say, and his groaning made me uncomfortable. Eventually, I gave up trying to talk, and I stopped sitting by him all together. I couldn't stand the look in his eyes. That empty stare devoid of intelligence. His nurse said that the pain and the meds affected his cognitive function. At this point, he lived a half-life, trapped between life and death, at the edge of the River Styx with no boat to carry him across. I secretly prayed for him to die. No one should live like that.

I felt like I was suffocating. All the death and dying, the tears and silence, drove me insane. The next morning, I grabbed Jacqueline and hopped in our rental. My mom stopped us outside and asked where we were going.

"Out," I said.

She was furious.

"What if he passes while you're out? What will you do then? What will I do?"

She started crying again. I couldn't take it. I told Jacqueline to get in the car and drove off.

"Maybe we should have stayed," Jacqueline said.

"I can't take that house. I'm not going to wait around for him to die. What's the point? He's already gone. Let him die, why tiptoe around it? If he passes now or ten days from now, he's still going."

"You don't want to have any regrets," she replied.

I kept driving. She was right, but I was stubborn. I knew I'd have regrets but that wasn't the point. I didn't want to be there when he died. I wanted to be as far away as possible.

It's what we all want, to distance ourselves from death. To push it off for as long as possible until it comes for us. It's why we sequester the dead and dying in clinical white buildings where death is spoken about in code. We can't stand to face the dead. In facing them, we face ourselves, and confronted with mortality, we dissociate. Cart the dead off, paint their faces and talk to them as if they're living, delude ourselves into thinking that we've coped. But none of us really face death, not really. That confrontation's left to the doctors and soldiers of the world, people we pay to confront death for us, intermediaries at best, victims at worst. In the end, death always feels unnatural, and maybe because it is, and men were made for more than dying. Maybe our longings, the ones expressed in poetry and art hint at a world beyond ours. Maybe death's only the messy middle, or in the end a violation of what should've been, life unending, Plato's immortal soul.

We drove to the beach, down a little one-lane dirt road, the same road my grandfather would drive down when I was a little and my mom and I wanted to go to the beach. It was a weekday, and the beach was all but empty, the one thing reminding us that it was still December. Christmas was only a few days away. Jacqueline offered to stay. If he didn't pass by then we'd fly out on the twenty-sixth so that she and I could spend some time with her family. Everything was moving so fast. We'd only been dating a few months, but things were speeding up. We didn't acknowledge it. Instead, we went along. Questioning it would mean questioning us, and neither of us was ready for that conversation.

We walked alongside the water hand in hand until we found a spot that felt right. I took off my sandals and wiggled my toes in the sand, feeling the rough grain rub against my soft feet. I winced; the sand was hot. I dug my feet a bit deeper. Here, the sand was cool. I sighed with relief. The waves were calm today. They moved slowly, lazily lapping at the shore like a cat licking its paw. Jacqueline laid out a towel and undressed. I followed suit and lifted my shirt over my head. I immediately felt the strength of the sun baking my skin. I sprayed myself down with sunscreen while Jacqueline covered herself in tanning oil. She would tan well. I usually burned.

We spent a few hours at the beach. I read while Jacqueline soaked up the sun. I asked if she wanted to go into the water, but she wasn't in the mood. I spent thirty minutes in the water, but without anyone to enjoy it with, the water was boring. When I got out, I dried off and suggested we leave. Staying still was a reminder of what we had to return to, and we'd been at the beach long enough. I was restless. I didn't want to go back to the house. I wanted to keep moving. Movement was life. Dead things laid still.

We shook off the sand and got back in the car. We moved again. We rolled the windows down and drove with the wind in our face. The air smelled like salt.

We stopped at a little open-air bar, a few miles out of Yauco. The bar was bright yellow and plastered with posters of half-naked models holding sweaty beer bottles. Jacqueline leaned over the bar and signaled the bartender. She ordered us two Medallas and a few seconds later we were sitting beneath a palm tree in red plastic chairs happily gulping down ice-cold beer. We ordered some food to offset the beer sloshing about in our empty stomachs. The sun began to make its descent. Our shadows stretched out behind us. We watched the sky turn golden; I told Jacqueline it reminded me of her hair. She smiled, got up from her seat, and sat on my lap. I felt the beer now. There was no difference between me and the sunset, both of us glowing, on fire, solar twins burning bright. I felt bold. I grabbed Jacqueline's waist, turned her around and kissed her. My lips lingered over hers, burning, glowing, and immolation of the best kind.

"What was that?" She asked.

Beer-fueled rhetoric spilled from my lips. I told her that I loved her, that I wanted to spend forever with her. I might've cried. But I desperately wanted it all to be true and knew deep down it wasn't. She said the same. We kissed again. The sun was about gone but I was still glowing. Then it was gone, the sun, the glow, the self-imposed amnesia. There was no more avoiding it, we had to head back.

The next day, Jacqueline and I woke up early and snuck out of the house to avoid another confrontation with my mother. We grabbed breakfast nearby, at a little cafe that served coffee out of someone's kitchen and drove to Ponce and to wander about the city. I took Jacqueline to all the places Abu took me as a kid, the old firehouse, the plaza, the museum. We had dinner in the city and finished the night walking around and eating passionfruit ice cream. When we got back to the house, my mother informed us that the church was coming to visit tomorrow and that it would mean a lot to Abu if we stayed. Despite how I felt, I couldn't say no, and so the next day Jacqueline and I spent the morning preparing the house for visitors.

They came around seven, crowding the house like a herd of wild boar, and I was already annoyed. The house, which for the last few days was quiet, was full of voices and the endless shuffling of feet as people milled about in the living room waiting for instructions. While they waited, we became the center of attention. A circle formed around my mother, Irma, and me. Everyone had something to say. Anecdotes, prayers, and even a few ill-timed condolences. I felt like telling them he wasn't dead, but they kept on talking and Jacqueline kept on translating. I itched for a cigarette. Since dating Jacqueline, I smoked less. She disapproved of the habit and wouldn't touch me when I smelled like smoke. I tried to sneak a smoke or two in on the sly, but the secrecy got tiring and smoking lost its joy.

There was a commotion by the door. The pastor had arrived. Now all the attention was focused on her, the "pastora." She was in her late fifties; she wore a black jacket with white slacks and three-inch high heels. The first thing I noticed was her make-up, her cheeks were almost as red as her lips. Her hair was something out of the eighties, all hairspray and volume, blown out and big. If you aren't familiar with Spanish Pentecostalism, the image of a female pastor might seem out of place, but female pastors weren't uncommon, and in the communities they served, they were held with special place of reverence; a religious leader, matriarch, and model woman all in one. She gathered the crowd together like a mother gathering her chicks.

"The scriptures say, 'when one of us is sick, call the elders and anoint them with oil.' Our brother Jose lies there, sick, beyond the help of medicine, and that's why we're here, to pray for our brother so that he may be made well."

There were a few nods and murmurs of affirmation. But that was just the beginning. After a few more scripture quotations and more words to similar effect, she led everyone into Abu's room. I followed behind them and ended up outside the room trapped in the hallway next to Jacqueline outside the bathroom.

Surrounded by all those people, Abu seemed even smaller. He smiled at the pastor and moved to lift his hand. The pastor came over and took out a little vial of oil from her purse, then with her forefinger, she marked his forehead with the sign of the cross. As if on cue, the congregation began to sing. At first, it was slow, like a lullaby, but then when they reached the chorus, the song kicked into another gear. Suddenly, they danced and clapped. People shouted and aimed their hands at Abu like crossing guards trying to stop the flow of traffic. It was madness, and soon the words of the song were lost, and the house was crowded with the confusing sound of conflicting voices, everyone saying and doing something different, a magic mixture of prayer and mismatched choruses.

But the louder they prayed, the angrier I got. He was dying, there was no miracle to be had, and even if there was, who would want to live like this, weak and bound to a bed, a shell of man, unable to speak or do? Sure, I believed in God, but this was too much. This wasn't about him, this was about them, and their inability to face the inevitable. If God wanted to save him, He would've done it by now, and if He didn't want to save him, that was His prerogative.

In that moment the irony was lost on me. I'd spent all week running from Abu, the dark specter that was his terminal diagnosis, and so like most people I projected my anger at myself onto them, raging at the well-meaning parishioners to absolve myself of my guilt.

I slipped into the bathroom and ran my hands under the scalding water until they burned. Abu was dying and there was nothing I could do about it. I slumped to the floor and laid myself out on the pink tile until the rage drained from my face. I emerged as they finished. Thankfully, they left quietly and once again the house was empty. Jacqueline tried to make small talk, but I was a million miles away, praying an altogether different kind of prayer:

"Lord, please take him, don't let him suffer."

Our trip was almost over. We woke up Christmas morning and sat around the coffee table in silence. Abu was still alive. But whether that was a gift or not, I was still unsure. We all felt it, the impossible weight of waiting. It hung over us like a storm cloud, one of those thick, bulbous, gray monstrosities loaded with rain, ready to burst and soak the earth beneath it, irrespective of those ready or not for rain. Jacqueline got up and turned on the radio and found a station playing Christmas music. It was Christmas, the thought had escaped me. There was no tree or gifts to be had, the house wasn't decorated, and we had no plans for dinner. This might well be Abu's last Christmas. I got up from the table and ran to my room to get ready. With Jacqueline in tow, I ran out to our rental and drove off to the little strip mall near the center of Yauco.

    The mall was nearly deserted and almost all the stores were closed, but as luck would have it, the K-mart was open and empty. The Christmas aisle was ransacked, bulbs and lights littered the floor, and fake snow fell off the shelves. I rummaged through the mess and found a neat little four-foot tree and a random assortment of trimmings. We went to the supermarket next and picked up whatever was left after the Christmas Eve rush. With our rental full, we drove back home and set up. By the afternoon, we'd transformed the living room into a mini winter wonderland. The mood in the house had lifted. Irma was warm and for the first time this trip, my mom smiled. She and Irma busied themselves with Jacqueline in the kitchen, laughing and joking as they prepared the food we bought for an early dinner.

    I got up from the living room and made my way to Abu's room. The Christmas music drifted in with me like a breeze breaking the silence that occupied his room. Abu stirred but didn't wake. I quietly closed the door and waited until I was sure that he couldn't hear me. Tiptoeing across the floor, I sat down on the chair Irma positioned by his bedside. It rocked as I sat down, the wicker bands holding it together creaking as it adjusted to my weight. I held still but Abu didn't move. His chest barely rose as he struggled to breathe. Perspiration trickled down his face despite the AC running at the far end of the room. He no longer looked like my grandfather. He looked like a wax figure at Madame Tussauds, a cheap imitation of the living, lifelike and lifeless all at once. I reached out my hand to touch him but at the last moment, I relented. There he was, my grandfather, breathing his last, and I could barely look at him. I screamed at my body to move but my arm stayed still. I told myself that this would be my last moment with him. I argued and reasoned, and implored myself to act, to do something, to express my love one final time, but I couldn't. I was trapped, my mind held prisoner by my will. There was so much I wanted to say but nothing came out. I felt myself getting up, moving to the door, leaving him there wheezing and barely breathing, but my feet kept moving. I was outside and anger and rage and humiliation flooded my face. I wanted to scream, to punish myself. But then I heard my father, his voice, and suddenly, I was a kid again with a bloody knee.

Walk it off.

Walk it off.

Then I was fine, and the pain was gone, pushed down beneath the bravado I inherited from my father and his father before him. I went back into the house. Smiled at Jacqueline as if nothing had happened. We were at the airport and up in the air and Abu was back in PR strapped to a bed, waiting for his grandson to say what needed to be said. But his grandson never came. I was back in NY, and I pushed Abu from my mind. New Year's Eve was a few days away, and Jacqueline and I made plans. Everything was normal. Life went on.

In many ways I'm still there, caught in the doorway, fighting a losing battle against my better nature, the words I should've said still caught in my throat, choking the truth out of me. What is it about me that keeps me from saying what needs to be said? Why do the right words never come, or better yet; why am I never brave enough to say them? Can it all be traced back to the bike ride, that early lesson in masking pain, or is this nature, who I am, a tortoise of sorts, shrinking into my shell when things get hard? Who ignores their dying grandfather? Who's that cruel? Maybe that's why I progress through life numb, preferring anesthesia to pain, even if it kills me—a fatal flaw in my character that leaves old men to die alone while I watch silently. Too dumb to say what's on my heart, and too scared to let myself feel the pain, knowing now I'll never get that moment back. Screaming, begging the gods that be to let me go back and let that young man know that regret hurts more and only grows over time, until all that's left are the memories of the moments you missed and the gnawing feeling in the back of your brain that says life would be different if you'd had the courage to say what needed to be said.

Chapter 9:

2014

My right eyelid does this thing when I'm tired or stressed. It starts twitching uncontrollably like a beetle struggling to get upright, wriggling and writhing, pulsing against my eye like a heart trying to keep pace with constricted arteries. It's my body's way of telling me that I'm at my wit's end, out of my depth, approaching a breakdown or worse. It comes and goes, but it's never gone for long, and the more I try to contain it, the worse it gets.

The twitching had started that morning. I'd put on my suit and tried to tie my tie in the finger-stained mirror of a musty motel room. Somewhere between the cross and the loop, my right eyelid moved on its own. I tossed down the tie in frustration and went to the sink to run cold water over my face. I gripped the edge of the sink with both hands and plunged my head under the water in hopes that the cold would shock my eyelid still, but as always, it didn't work, it just got worse. There I was in the mirror, face soaked, eye moving, disheveled and tieless, doing my best to keep my breakfast down. The decades-old smell of cigarette smoke was unrelenting. It pressed in around me like a noxious cloud and sent my head spinning. I felt my stomach lurch and I nearly gagged. I needed fresh air.

    Abandoning my tie, I grabbed my room key and closed the door behind me. It was early but it was already hot. I took off my suit jacket and unbuttoned my shirt. Sweat pooled under my arms. I followed the street to a small cafe on the corner of the road and without checking if it was open or not, went inside in hopes they had an AC. They didn't. All they had were two box fans in the far corner of the room working overtime to expel the heat. They worked, but only if you sat right next to them and let them buzz directly in your ear. It was better than nothing. I ordered a cold beer and sat at the bar with my jacket slung over the seat next to mine. My head had stopped spinning, but my eye still twitched. I held the bottle to my forehead and for the first time that morning, I let myself breathe.

My phone rattled against the countertop. I lifted it up and read the text message that scrolled across a picture of me and Jacqueline at a New Year's Eve party, both of us a little drunk, wearing numbered shades and holding a bottle of champagne. I needed to change that picture. My mother had texted me asking for an ETA. She was nervous, but why the rush, we had all day? I texted her back and let her know that I'd be there in a bit.

I looked at the picture again. We seemed so happy there, the whole world in front of us ready for the taking. But then again, we'd gotten pretty good at pretending. Things came to a head after my birthday in February. We were supposed to meet for breakfast, but when we met up, something seemed off. She wouldn't look at me, and when I went in to kiss her, she turned her head the other way. I asked her what was wrong, and she asked if we could go somewhere private to talk. We got as far as the park across the street from my house and sat down on a bench in front of an old war memorial, the soldiers' names worn away by rain and the encroaching moss. She started to tell me that she was unhappy and from the rasp in her voice, I could tell she'd been crying. She told me that there was someone else. I should've been shocked, and angry, but it came as no surprise, and I couldn't blame her. For months, we'd tried to pretend that the cracks weren't there.

She and the guy had met before we left for PR. She said that she'd wanted to tell me then and that after our trip, she tried to cut it off. But in the end, she couldn't. She'd thought I'd notice, but if I'm being honest, I didn't. After our trip to PR, I withdrew. Life was a blur. One day blended into the next and I spent most of my time alone or at the bar or with my friend Janiece who was the only person I was ever honest with.

I asked her why now. She said that a part of her still loved me and wanted to make it work. She kept talking, but I wasn't listening, I read the monument, looking over the last legible names etched into the stone. I imagined their faces. Young men, ready to take on the world, only to be gunned down by some German weapon, their decaying bodies used as fertilizer for foreign soil. But at least they died for something, and maybe dying young was easier than living to be old for nothing.

"Ryan! Are you listening?"

Her eyes were red and puffy.

"Are you going to say anything?"

She leaned in, her face almost next to mine. She searched me with her eyes, looking for tears, signs of life, but my face was blank. My eyes were dry. Her lips quivered while mine were sealed shut. Looking back, I think she wanted me to fight for her, or at least to yell at her, do something that screamed I cared. I tried. I tried to find the words and come up with a response. But there was nothing there, and I realized then that I didn't love her, or maybe I'd simply forgotten how. Either way, I couldn't give her what she needed. I leaned over and kissed her. It was all the goodbye I could muster. We met up a week later to try and salvage what we could. Nothing worked and waking up in bed together only clarified what we both knew to be true—this was goodbye.

I looked up at the clock behind the counter. It was 9:45 AM. I finished my beer, left my money beneath the empty bottle, thanked the owner and walked back to the motel, got in the rental car parked out front, threw my jacket in the backseat and blasted the AC. My phone rang again, it was my mother, asking where I was. I told her I was on my way. Why the rush, I thought, we have all day. I hung up, put the car in drive, and drove off. There was no more putting it off. It was time for Abu's funeral.

The funeral home was small, white, and sandwiched between the post office and a boarded-up hair salon. At one-point colorful tiles decorated the front, but most of them were cracked and the ones that were left were bright but indiscernible, a random assortment of tropical hues—bright blues, yellows, and greens. The flower beds beneath the windows were empty and the glass in the frames cracked and taped over to prevent the rain from getting in. I tried to make out the sign above the door, but the paint was faded and all I could read were the words "funeraria" and what looked like a white cross and a date.

The doors were open. My mother, Irma, and Irma's sister, Hilda, were already inside. I walked up to the door and peered inside. It was quiet. The lights were off. Thin beams of sunlight peeked through the shutters, but even these seemed cloudy and muted, obscured by the dancing dust mites suspended between the beams. Over in the corner, tucked away between the shadows, was a statue of a saint, pale-faced and hallowed, encased in finger-smudged glass like a circus clown at a freakshow. His eyes were hollow, the paint rubbed raw, leaving only empty white where his eyes should've been. A fitting patron for a funeral home; a lifeless husk as blind as the dead. As I looked into the whites of his eyes, I saw myself, empty and hollow, a shell of regret; should'ves, would'ves, and could'ves clinging to me like the blue shawl wrapped around the saint's shoulders, lifeless eyes looking back at me, showing me myself. I dug out a piece of paper from my pocket. It was wrinkled and poorly folded, the edges unaligned and crooked like misplaced valleys mistakenly cut into the earth. I didn't have the heart to open it. It was Abu's eulogy. My mother and Irma had asked me to write it, to speak on behalf of the family at the funeral. I put off writing it until I got on the plane and even then, nothing came. The words were still stuck in my throat. Instead of saying what I needed to say, the speech read like a Hallmark greeting card. Beautiful, sure, but lifeless and plastic, a plaster saint made up to look real.

 The door to the funeral parlor was closed. A sign with my grandfather's name and his picture hung limply in a copper frame, unnecessary, as the funeral home was small, and we were the only service scheduled for that evening. The funeral was set to start at 6 PM but we had to be there early, to wait with the body, and greet the well-wishers who trickled in during the day to pay their respects. I pushed open the walnut brown doors. They were heavy and moved slowly, though I imagined the weight was all in my head and what I really felt was the crushing weight of the inevitable.

 The doors opened and a blast of cool air hit me, and for a moment I stood between the parlor and the lobby, hot and cold, deciding if I should turn back and suffer the heat or endure the cold and lifeless body beyond the doors. I chose the latter. The doors closed with a bang and the remaining hot air was sucked out of the room. Irma and my mom were at the far end of the room, huddled together with Hilda between them. They were still, save for the slight movement of their shoulders as they sniffled and reached for tissues to wipe away their tears. In front of them was the casket. It was red and glossy, probably oak. It was stationed between two large bundles of flowers that stood like sentries, unmoving and unconcerned. Between the red wood and the cream-colored interior lay Abu.

 From where I stood, he looked like himself, serious and quiet with his wisps of white hair combed and parted to the right side of his face. He looked like he was sleeping, all he was missing was a steady rise in his chest and the sound of air struggling to make its way past his clogged nostrils. But the illusion broke as I made my way forward. What distance obscured, proximity revealed. He was impossibly still. His face, usually tanned, was sharp and white like a marble statue trying its best to imitate life. I stood above his body and took it all in—the makeup on his face, the slight wrinkle in his tie, the faux-gold cufflinks I bought him for Father's Day when I was eight, the Bible by his side. Every detail etched into my mind, already overriding my memories of him healthy and alive.

I sat next to my mother. She leaned her head against my shoulder and sobbed all over again. I thought to put my arm around her, but my body wouldn't respond. I felt her tears work their way through my shirt, leaving a wet blotch above my heart. I shivered. The room was cold, and for a moment, I imagined what it was like to be dead. Cold, stiff, stuck in a box, unable to move my lips. Listening to the whimpering and wailing, a voyeur from the other side, destined to observe but never interfere, surrounded by well-wishers speaking about me in the past tense as if I wasn't there.

The door opened. It was the funeral director. An unassuming man with no definable features, like a lump of clay roughly resembling a person. Given his profession, it made sense. His job was to disappear, to appear when needed, an invisible hand guiding grieving families as they laid their loved ones to rest. He walked over to us with his head bent low, eyes stuck to his toes. When he looked up, it was to address us, and even then, his eyes never met ours. He gave us the illusion that he looked at us when he looked past us.

I don't know why I noticed this. But grief tends to leave behind funny details. It's as if our brains know that we can take only so much pain. Unbeknownst to us, our brains work to avert our gaze and distract us from the pain; like pinching your thigh while the dentist cleans your teeth or telling a joke before resetting someone's shoulder. For a moment, there's relief, but the trick only lasts so long, and in the end, the agony persists worse now, because we had a moment of ignorant bliss.

The door opened again. The funeral director was joined by a small group of elderly women. They were from the church. I recognized them from my grandfather's party. They shuffled into the room and surrounded Irma and my mother and smothered them in hugs, kisses, and condolences. They did the same with me. Though I couldn't understand what they said, I smiled and nodded and that seemed to sate them. They turned around and surrounded the casket. The waterworks began almost immediately. Their sniffling turned into wailing, tissues were passed around, makeup was fixed, and they were out the door. Their absence filling the room was the same sort of silence you notice after a storm.

The rest of the day went pretty much the same. People passed through every thirty minutes or so, never staying longer than a few minutes, each of them doing a variation of the same routine. I moved from where I was sitting to the back of the room. Whenever the door opened, I did my best to make myself invisible. I couldn't take the pity. The sad smiles, the sorrys, the hugs, they felt empty. What could they say? Sure, they were sorry, but when we say sorry, we're mostly saying that we're sorry it's you, and saying, thank God it wasn't us.

I needed some air. I excused myself and left my mom and Irma in the chapel. I exited the lobby and stood outside. For once, the heat felt good. I let the sun beat down on me and sighed with relief as the last bits of artificial cold left my body. My stomach growled. I looked down at my watch. It was already 2:00 PM. I texted my mom and asked if she and Irma were hungry. She said they were fine; they would eat later when the funeral was done. I didn't argue. I couldn't. I didn't have the energy.

I got in my car and drove to the McDonalds down the road. It stuck out like a sore thumb against the backdrop of old Spanish colonial buildings and the lush green of the palm trees. The inorganic yellow and red stained the countryside, colonization of a different kind, a reminder that for all the island's enchantment, a red, white, and blue shadow still loomed. But none of that dawned on me then. I was hungry and exhausted, lost in a grief-induced delirium. I was like a zombie, I couldn't cry or speak, all I could muster was a grim face and an unapproachable glare. I desperately wanted to cry, to scream, to shed tears and wail, but it wouldn't come. I felt nothing.

They said denial was a part of the grieving process, but I wasn't sure utter apathy was. We always felt something, even if only briefly, but ever since I'd broken up with Jacqueline and got the news that Abu died, I was an emotional void. Anesthetized and numb, as cold as Abu's dead hands. I was the same way when my dad left. The anger came later, but even then, it was cool and calculating, a means to an end, a way to exact revenge against my absentee father. As I sat there, sitting in a ghastly, purple plastic booth, I tried to remember the last time I felt anything. I felt like a voyeur, watching my life as it happened from somewhere outside myself.

I sat down with my order and picked at my fries. They were warm and crisp, but at that moment they tasted cold and soggy. I pushed the tray away from me. I wasn't hungry. I reached into my pocket and pulled out my speech. The paper was damp with sweat. I laid it out and tried to straighten out the wrinkles. The ink was splotchy in places, but my handwriting was still legible. I ran through the lines in my head. It was good. It captured well Abu's life, work, accomplishments, and personality, but as I read it over again, I realized how impersonal it was. There was no mention of our relationship and I only mentioned myself when I listed the family he left behind. Anyone with a decent knowledge of his life could've written this. I'd tried to write something personal, but I never got past the first line. I read through the speech again. Satisfied I was familiar with the lines, I folded it up and put it back in my pocket. Impersonal or not, it would have to do.

    I dumped my uneaten food in the garbage and walked back to my car, put the AC on blast, slumped in my chair and closed my eyes. It was quiet. The rush of the day was drowned out by the soft whooshing of the air and the rumbling of the idling car engine. The funeral started at six. The right thing to do would be to go back to the funeral home and support my mother, but I couldn't take another three hours trapped in that funeral home. I didn't know where I was going, and my phone was almost dead. I should really head back, I thought to myself. But even as I put the car in gear, I knew that I wasn't going back, not yet anyways. The car peeled out of the parking lot. I was on autopilot. All I knew was that I needed to drive and feel the air on my face. I needed space.

    The car was gone, I was gone, all that existed was movement and light, the rumbling of that ancient beast that propelled me forward and the sun sparkling off the ocean. A giant blue diamond shimmering in the hand of an invisible jeweler, turning the gem this way and that to get a better look, waves moving like facets under a headlamp as if waiting their final appraisal.

    We were motionless, and the sun seemed frozen in place, and time was unmoving, unable to go forward or back. I sat overlooking the ocean, the car parked on the sand, ignoring my vibrating phone.

This must be what drowning feels like, at least after the struggle, when all you can do is give into the weight of the water, close your eyes, and resign yourself to death. Everything is still, there's no time, there's only that moment, and the perfect serenity that comes with surrender. We spend our whole lives fighting, waging war against the inevitable. We claw and scratch like big cats fighting over a corpse. We run and move and jump, thinking that if we keep moving, we'll never grow still enough to die, all of us caught up in the lie that living is movement and death, a sudden end, the motionless end of our long march. But maybe death is a blessing, and the stillness is exactly what we need. Maybe I should've taken off my shoes, walked into the waves and let the gentle current rock me still.

The phone buzzed again. It was late. The service was about to start. It wasn't my time, not yet at least. I dusted off my feet and slid them back into my shoes. The grains I missed dug into my soles as I gave the car a little gas. A small act of penance.

When I arrived at the funeral home, the sun was already gone and there was a line of cars parked outside. I turned the corner and parked the car next to a hydrant. Before getting out I did my best to fix myself. I tucked in my shirt and ran my hands through my hair in a botched attempt to tame my wild curls. When I thought I looked presentable enough, I got out of the car and lit a cigarette. I took two or three long draws, enough to get the nicotine going. I patted my leg. The speech was there, and with nothing left to help me bide my time, I turned the corner and walked into the funeral home.

The lobby was packed. Men and women milled about conversing in hushed tones, some of them catching up for the first time in years. I recognized a few of them. There was my tio Eusebio who grew up with my mom. Despite being younger than my mom, he had bright white hair. He told me that he began to gray in his teens, and since turning eighteen I nervously looked in the mirror for any signs that I inherited his genes. He and his wife Esther were the only family we really talked to. They lived a few minutes away from us, right off Springfield Blvd and Hillside Avenue. When my parents divorced, my mother cut a lot of people off. But they remained a steady presence in our lives. They didn't have any children. They tried, of course, but that had ended in tragedy. With no children of his own, he became a surrogate father, checking in on me now and then, and stepping in when I became too much for my mom. Funnily enough, he wasn't really my uncle, he was my second cousin. Though I didn't put two and two together until I was about thirteen and realized that my mom was, in fact, an only child.

Standing next to them was a big, burly, serious man. His name was Tato. My knowledge was vague on the details surrounding our relationship. All I knew was that Abu practically raised him. He was a permanent fixture in our family. He showed up to everything. After Abu, he took on the mantle of patriarch and had even paid for my mother's flights for the funeral. We weren't particularly close. He was a retired NYPD lieutenant, serious and grim, and always at distance. He worked for the NYPD during the 80s. He'd been shot once and stabbed twice doing undercover narcotics. My mother always pushed me to try and connect with him. But we had nothing in common. He was dependable and that was enough.

The funeral director motioned for us to enter the parlor. It was dark. The sun was pretty much gone. The only source of light came from the lamps on the wall behind the casket. We shuffled in one at a time. The room was filled with sniffling and quiet whispers. The easy conversation that flowed so easily in the lobby was reduced to a small, hesitant whisper. I made my way up the center aisle and took my place next to my mother. I expected her to chide me, to ask where I'd been, but she barely noticed I was there. After a few minutes of sitting silently in the dark, Abu's pastor got up and invited us to stand. She started to lead us in a chorus. Her voice was hoarse and deep, like a smoker's, and would give out whenever she tried to hit the high notes. Eventually, the collective voice of the crowd drowned hers out. There was something comforting about losing yourself in a crowd of loud voices. Suddenly, you weren't just yourself. You were no one and everyone. Caught up in an infinite embrace, unable to tell where you ended, and they began. I didn't know the words, I didn't need to, this was a moment beyond language, beyond comprehension. All of us together, united in grief, reminding one another that loss was both particular and universal. We got to the last note and held on as long as we could. Everyone sat down. We were individuals again.

The pastor said very little. She offered her condolences and led us in a prayer. It was only after she said Amen that I remembered that I was next. I pulled out the crumpled speech from my pants pocket and unfolded it against my leg to work out the creases. Most of it was still legible, save for the few small places where the ink had smudged. The pastor motioned at me. I got up. The podium was beside the casket. I stood behind it and placed the paper down. I realized then that I'd written my speech in English. Besides my mother and my family visiting from New York, no one would understand a word. If I hadn't been standing in front of everyone I would've laughed. There I was, ready to pour out my heart, and almost no one would hear it. I smiled. Abu would've found that funny too.

"Friends and family. Today we lay to rest Jose Rivera, my grandfather, or as I called him, Abu. Abu was many things but above all, he desperately cared about people. His life was a living sacrifice, a daily denial of self-interest for the sake of the good of others. Many of you here today are beneficiaries of his kindness, his patience, and his ability to see the latent potential in any person regardless of their current situation. Abu wasn't traditionally religious by any stretch of the imagination. I never saw him pray or read the Bible, all I knew was that he attended church and helped people. That was the core of Abu's religion, a desire to help, to do the good work left undone by the busy and the apathetic. It's this self-giving that marked Abu's life. With his passing, it's incumbent on us to continue his legacy and forge a way forward without him, to live the sort of lives worthy of his legacy. Thank you."

I folded the paper up and returned to my seat.

Looking back over the words, I realize now that I said nothing about my relationship with Abu. I think it was easier to simply speak about him than to acknowledge what he meant to me. I was still standing at a distance, outside myself, playing the voyeur in my own life.

My mother leaned over and grabbed my arm. It was the only thank you she could muster. The pastor returned to the podium and brought the service to a close. One by one people filtered out of the room until my mother, Irma, Abu, and I remained. The day ended like it began, alone in a dark room with a cold corpse, silent, save for the whirring of the AC and the low hum of fluorescent bulbs. I got up first, then Irma and lastly my mother. Tato waited outside. Irma and my mother got in his car. I watched them pull off. The car faded from view. The street was dark. I got in my car, rolled down the window, and lit a cigarette. The speech was still in my pocket. I looked it over one last time, crumpled it up, and tossed it out the window. The car rumbled to life. The road was dark and again, I was alone. I was always alone, trapped somewhere outside myself, desperately trying to claw my way in.

The next morning, I woke up, got dressed, and drove back to the funeral home for the burial. A long line of cars sat idling behind a long black hearse, rumbling like a band of angry bees trapped in a jar. The funeral director was outside handing out pink tabs that read "funeral" for people to stick under their windshield. I went inside. My mother and Irma were huddled behind my uncle while they waited for the funeral director to finish up out front. No one said much. There was nothing left to say. This was the end. The last goodbye.

The funeral director ushered us into the room. The casket was closed. The funeral director pulled Tato, Chevy, a young man from the church, and me to the side and walked us over to the casket. Together, we rolled the casket into the lobby, and once by the door, we picked it up and put it on our shoulders. I felt the weight of the casket shoot through my body. I repositioned myself, careful not to make any sudden moves. Once we were all adjusted, we moved forward. Making our way slowly toward the hearse, we felt the weight of the casket afresh with every step. The Via Dolorosa. The way of suffering. Christ suffocating under the weight of the cross, us suffering under the weight of a casket, carrying death on our shoulders like farmers hauling hay. Each of us walked our predestined path. We laid the casket in the hearse. The casket was gone but the weight remained. I got in my car and pulled it behind the hearse. My mother would ride with Tato and Irma. She wasn't speaking to me. She couldn't. The funeral director gave a thumbs up to the driver and the hearse sputtered to life. We moved slowly, following the winding roads out to the cemetery on the edge of the town. It wasn't a long drive. After ten minutes or so, the hearse stopped at an iron gate. In the distance, I saw rows of white stone sticking up from the earth. In Puerto Rico, the dead were placed in tombs and walled in with cement and mortar in case of flooding. Shortly after moving back to Puerto Rico, Abu purchased a plot. Even then, a part of him knew he'd die here.

The hearse rolled to a stop. I shut off my car and got out. The funeral director told us that the tomb was a five-minute walk away. We followed the funeral director to the plot across a dirt path between the tombs. Some were white, brand new, freshly erected to welcome the soon-to-be dead. The rest were dirty, covered in the dust kicked up by the wind that came in from over the sea. A few were covered in flowers and knickknacks. A saint candle here, a whisky bottle there, evidence that despite the years, these people were still loved. There were those with dead flowers and shattered glass. These hadn't seen any visitors for quite some time. No one missed them.

In the end, all we'll be is a memory. A fleeting image, an impression in the minds of those who knew us. Looking out at a cemetery, you can't help but wonder how you'll be remembered. Will someone leave you flowers, or will the wind and rain eventually erase your name?

I looked back at the procession behind me. This was Abu, now. Alive in us, even if only briefly.

We came to a stop. The tomb was made of white marble. Thin black rivers ran across its surface. It sparkled when the sun hit it right. On the face of the tomb was Abu's name. Jose Rivera: husband, father, grandfather. It was simple. Like him. We lowered the casket onto the device that would lower it into the tomb and watched as the cemetery attendants maneuvered it over the tomb's black marble mouth.

We gathered around the casket, all of us dressed in black despite the heat. Roses were passed around, their petals drooping, desperately clinging to their stems. One by one, we passed the casket and laid our flowers to rest, each of us whispering something, forgetting for a moment that he couldn't hear us.

After everyone had passed the casket, we sang a final chorus.

"Tengo paz en mi ser. Tengo paz, tengo paz en mi ser."

It is well with my soul. It is well, it is well with my soul.

The crowd retreated and I was left alone with the cemetery workers. Slowly, they lowered the casket down into the marble tomb. No pomp, no circumstance, no final chorus. Just the creaking of metal and the grunts of underpaid men. To them, it was another box. One of the many they'd lowered into the earth, a thing to be checked off a to-do list before their boss got back from lunch. Something that meant so much to me, meant nothing to them. It was just another box, and as I watched the casket settle at the bottom of the tomb, I knew for myself that it was just another box, the body just another body, and this island was just another island. The enchantment was gone. Abu was gone. I knew that I wouldn't return. There was nothing left for me here. All I had left were memories and all the things I should've said.

The workers looked restless. They had work to do, caskets to lift and tombs to fill. I left them to it. I heard the creak of the crank as they lowered the casket down and the subtle thud when it finally found its berth. I turned around in time to see them slide the lid over the open tomb. It slid into place with a satisfying thump. The deed was done, the tomb was shut, and as I walked back to my car, I imagined myself lying at the bottom of one of those tombs, surrounded by darkness and sequestered from sound. The thought was oddly comforting. In a way, death was like returning to the womb, the only safe place we knew before we were thrust out into the world. In the end, we all longed to return to that security, that void devoid of pain, and if death was but a brief respite before our resurrection, the tomb was but a womb preparing us for birth.

The house was crowded. People milled about on the porch in small groups, balancing drinks and heavy plates of food. Most of them laughed. The conversation flowed freely now, as if the burial gave them permission to shake off the grief clinging to their clothes. I walked through the crowd with my head down. I wasn't ready for casual conversation. Inside, the house was quieter. My mother and Irma sat quietly talking at the kitchen table, surrounded by piles of aluminum trays, enough food to last them a few days. My mother wanted to stay another week, but I had no plans to join her. I wanted to put all this behind me and get back to my life. I'd already booked a flight for later that day. Of course, my mother was disappointed, but I was too selfish to care, and I was tired of pretending to be sad when I was numb. I'd already packed my bags and checked out of my motel, and my plan was to hide out in my old room until the crowd dispersed and I could leave without much fuss from my mom.

But before I could slip away to my room, Irma called me over.

"Your Abu left you a few things. There in his office, on his desk."

I'd never been in Abu's office. It was the only part of the house he'd kept to himself. When I walked in, it was musty and dark. A thin layer of dust clung to his desk. Papers were strewn across the desk's surface. Abu wasn't the neatest, he preferred organized chaos. From the looks of things, Irma hadn't had the heart to tidy up his room. I looked through the papers. It was mostly bills and old notes. His handwriting was like mine, gibberish to the untrained eye. On top of all the scattered papers were a manila envelope and a black leather Bible pinned with a yellow sticky note with my name written in shaky capital letters.

I opened the envelope first. A silver ring fell onto the table. Little arrows ran along its sides, surrounding a blue stone, a bit of ocean trapped in a silver cage. Abu never really wore it. When he did wear it, it was when Irma wasn't around. I think it was a gift from my grandmother, which would explain Irma's disdain for it. I picked it up and held it in my hand. There was a bit of weight to it. I slipped the ring onto my ring-finger. It was too big, and even on my middle finger it threatened to slide off. I took the silver chain I wore and placed the ring on the chain, around my neck. I felt the cold silver against my chest, like air on an open wound, pressing against my bare skin like a brand, at once hot and cold. All my repressed emotions condensed into a piece of metal weighing less than three grams. I fell into his chair. The leather was supple, worn in from use, the arms nicked and scratched from where he'd pick at the fraying leather. I sunk into the chair like it was Abu's arms and allowed the weight of the past few days to wash over me. There, alone in his office, I sat silently, remembering his voice, his face, carefully categorizing each feature.

Of course, now I barely remember his voice. Time dilutes memory. It robs it of its clarity. Vivid impressions are replaced by dull and scattered detail—a stray scent of cologne, a peculiar phrase. People and places are reduced to a fog, like seeing through cloudy glasses or getting caught in a snowstorm. You can see, but barely. Objects lose their clarity. All you have left are shapes and vague impressions. Back then, I still believed in the power of memory, but even then, only a few hours after his burial things began to lose shape.

His Bible lay unopened across from me. It was falling apart. The spine was bent, pages were dislodged, and the leather was torn. I opened it up to find that the pages were covered in notes, little doodles with streaks of highlighter yellow cutting off verses from the rest of the text. It was odd. I never saw him read it. But looking down at that tattered KJV, all evidence pointed to the contrary. I flipped through the pages. Each page was the same. A thousand different notes and marks lined the pages like hieroglyphics. I tried to read them, but I couldn't make heads or tails of Abu's handwriting compressed between margins and written in an odd mix of Spanish and English. I turned the page again. Ecclesiastes three. The whole chapter was surrounded by a hundred concentric circles written in red pen, a whirlpool of ink pressing in around the lines, drawing me towards the page like a gravity well, inescapable and all consuming:

"There is a time for everything."

"A time to be born and a time to die... A time to weep... A time to mourn."

Abu's final words. The last we'd share. Alone, facing the page, the highlighter yellow framed the words like a halo.

Chapter 10:

The Landing

The plane rolled to a stop. We were here. I stepped out into the aisle, grabbed my bag from the overhead bin, and slung it over my shoulder.

"You okay?"

I looked down at my wife, Janiece. She stared up at me with her brown eyes, sitting with her legs crossed, dark skin peeking out from beneath where her shirt was cropped short, above her belly. There was a time when we were just friends. Then she wanted me to be with Morgan. She loved the idea of me dating her best friend. One time, she invited us both out to dinner, only to cancel after we'd already sat down at a table for two. But for all her meddling, Morgan refused to settle down; at least with me, that was. Despite that, Janiece and I remained friends and in college, we were best friends. She worked at a Barnes and Noble on Utopia Turnpike, down the road from where I went to school. We'd meet up between classes on her breaks and sit at the cafe and work on our homework and read and vent about our love lives. It only took her a few weeks to see that Jacqueline and I weren't meant to be. I ignored her, and she ignored me when I told her that a long-distance relationship with an emotionally absent man wouldn't work.

It took time. But we eventually realized that there was more to us than met the eye. Too many near kisses, too many lingering looks, a lifetime of friendship evolving into love. We were married two years after we graduated from school. I worked at a church and thought that I could make a difference, but then that was over, and we were both disillusioned. Somehow, we survived and made it to five years. She was the first person I showed my writing to, my first editor and reader. She believed in me when no one else did. I didn't know if I'd have done the same for her, she was certainly a better wife than I was a husband. I tried, but I thought I failed far more often than she let on.

"Are you okay?" She asked again, this time grabbing my hand and forcing my gaze towards her.

She had that look on. She knew something was up. She always sensed when there was a change in my mood.

"I'm fine," I replied.

It was a lie. She knew it and I knew it. But she didn't press it.

With our bags in hand, we followed the slow-moving line off the plane and into the airport. Her parents were at the terminal waiting for us. Together, we made our way to baggage claim to pick up our luggage.

The carousel was crowded. Our plane was overbooked, and every seat was accounted for. Most of them were tourists in tropical shirts, wide-brimmed sun hats, and a wide assortment of shades. They were impatient. Itchy to get their money's worth, watching their watches like stock trends, sucking their teeth when their bags didn't pass by. I envied them, their restless excitement, overstuffed bags, and unfamiliarity. The baggage they brought fit neatly in carry-ons and armored luggage bags, all of it folded and squared away in convenient piles, leaving their minds empty and free, ready to relax and unwind in the Caribbean sun. The ease of a tourist, that was what I wanted, the ignorance that came with distance, and where the only associations that mattered were the ones that reminded you of fun and hours spent sprawled out under the sun.

Our bags came round the carousel, peeking out from beneath a monogram Gucci bag. I tried to ignore it, but Janiece saw it and tugged at my arm to go and grab it. I debated letting it go again for another spin, saying I missed it and didn't want to chase it down. But Janiece would know that something was up. She already knew that something bothered me, and any lie that I told to the contrary would only make her press me more.

Despite myself, I grabbed our bags and followed my in-laws out into the parking lot.

I felt the sun first. Those warm beams like hands caressing your skin, enveloping every inch of you until where you end and the sun begins seemed irrelevant, and anything below seventy degrees was a distant memory.

While my father-in-law finished up at the register, I loaded our rental and opened the doors to let out the hot air. It didn't make a difference. The car was still stuffy and warm, and even with the AC at full blast, it took about twenty minutes to expel the last bit of heat.

In the time it took for the car to cool down, we'd arrived at a guest house overlooking the Atlantic. It was nothing like my grandfather's house. The house was stout and square, with straight lines and neat edges. Floor-to-ceiling windows looked out onto the backyard, where the grass was trimmed and impossibly green. An inground pool jutted out onto a small vista, from which the sea in the distance stood still as glass, and the horizon looked like it was drawn on the sky with a ruler and pen. The inside of the house looked like the inside of the MOMA. Egg-shaped sofas and an oblong reading desk dotted the white interior. An off-brand Pollock hung in the dining room. It was a museum to modernism: colorless and streamlined, the exact opposite of the island outside its doors. It was why tourists like us liked it. Like a hermetic seal, it sealed us off from the real life of the island and its residents, letting us believe for a moment, like those European settlers before us, that we were in virgin, untapped land. This was complicated when your family had roots on the island. You were forced to walk between two worlds, the world of the mindless vacationer, empty-headed and carefree, and the world of the prodigal son coming home, wondering if he still had a place in his father's house.

My wife called me into the kitchen. She held an open bottle of wine in her hand. The bottle was cold. Little beads ran down the side and onto her brown skin like early morning dew on a bed of soil. She was happy. Her smile split her face in two. She'd turned the music on and swayed in time to the beat, balancing the bottle and her glass in her hands, spilling neither. She set the bottle down and poured the rosé into a crystal flute. I smiled and thanked her and took a sip. It was sweet and flowery. A citrus tang lingered on the tongue. It was the kind of wine you drank on vacation. Smooth enough to lose track of while you drank under the Caribbean sun.

I followed her out to the backyard. Her parents swung lazily on a hammock underneath a set of palm trees.

Abu had a hammock.

Abu. He lingered behind the hammock like a ghost, a shadow plastered against the skyline, darkening the bright colors of the backyard with his inescapable presence.

I poured myself a second glass. The drink swirled in my cup like a whirlpool. I stared at the bottom of the glass until it was empty, and his shade was a lingering notion in the back of my mind. I knew I'd have to face him eventually, but at that moment, I wasn't quite ready for those memories.

We spent the next few days driving around the island, first driving through Rio Grande and then down PR-3 to Fajardo where we visited some of Janiece's relatives. We did all the things tourists do: walked Old San Juan, visited El Yunque, and laid out on the tourist-ridden beaches that bordered the Atlantic, populated by bare-skinned Europeans and young Americans looking to enjoy the "foreign sands" of the Puerto Rican shore.

This was a Puerto Rico I didn't recognize, and for the first time I realized I was more Puerto Rican than I was led to believe. Like a homebody who'd never left the main street of their hometown, my knowledge of PR was limited. I knew only Yauco and the part of Ponce we went to for dinner. I knew those streets like the back of my hand. My Puerto Rico was there, and, in many ways, it was home: familiar and comforting. All these years I considered myself an outsider, an interloper, Puerto Rican in name only, but surrounded by the French moms with their dune-buggy carriages and the white college freshmen looking for Pina Coladas and authenticity, I realized I had nothing in common with them. I wasn't a tourist or a stranger, I was home. But as quickly as the epiphany arrived, it was overshadowed by the specter of regret, that same specter that had followed me off the island after Abu's death and for years barred my way back.

I'd lost the right to call PR home the day I left Abu to die without saying a word.

The next day, my in-laws offered us the car. They were going to see some relatives who offered to pick them up and bring them back to our rental home. A day alone on the island was exactly what we needed.

Almost all newlyweds walk into marriage believing in a pipedream. We're inundated with fantasies. All we know are the endings of rom-coms, which tend to never show the bitter work of longevity, but leave us at the beginning, when everything's good and easy and time hasn't had its chance to chip away at the facade we call the honeymoon phase, a tropical backdrop conveniently draped over the baggage we carry. No one tells newlyweds about the hard times, and if they do, we never listen. Those are problems for other people, we say, those hopeless dopes trapped in loveless marriages. We tend to think we're special and that problems plaguing others will never touch us. We're ignorant and stupid, and it only takes a few months to realize that those hopeless dopes were right and that we, for all our "love," are hopelessly unprepared to actually love.

We'd learned our lesson the hard way. Five years in, and we still tried to hit our stride. We loved each other, but things were strained. Empty bank accounts and two years of pandemic revealed the cracks we'd so expertly covered before. Those cracks grew into chasms.

Getting alone was a start.

It's amazing how you can live with someone and go days without truly seeing them. Life gets busy. You get caught up in the hustle, unaware that time's slipping away, and before you know it, weeks go by without any real conversation. You're like a swimmer, mindlessly going through the strokes, trying your best to keep your head above water, hoping that you have enough strength to keep going. No one ever tells you to get out of the pool. They tell you to keep swimming, as if all we know is motion. Stillness, for all its lauded virtues, is rejected in favor of hurry, and the relentless feeling that those things we've left undone are necessary to our being, forgetting that doing is all but one part of the human person, and that being is doing's better brother.

It was time to get out of the pool.

At first, we drove aimlessly, following the coastline of the island where the sapphire waves stretched themselves out beyond the horizon. About an hour in, we stopped to eat in Arecibo, a little place by the water, where we drank, ate mofongo, and enjoyed the sun from the safety of our umbrella. We got back in the car with two cold beers hidden in paper bags jammed into the center console, the brown bottles barely peeking above the end of the bags.

It took me about two miles to realize we drove south. We were on the PR-10, cutting through the island headed towards Ponce. On either side of us, the island rose in jagged bumps and green hills. The road twisted and turned as we went up and down the sides of the mountains, the black asphalt running this way and that like the river Styx running through the underworld. We passed Ponce and merged onto the PR-52, the Caribbean Sea dancing on our right, calmer than her older sister the Atlantic, her waters steady and smooth like a plane of silver glass.

We were in Yauco, passing the town square, and the shopping center after that. The old cemetery with its elegiac graffiti was covered in fresh paint, replacing the worn-out murals of my childhood. New names and faces covered the walls in vibrant hues, the old ones, the ones I recognized, gone—a second death. But for the first time, I saw the murals in a different light. They weren't memorials, those were for tombstones. These were celebrations, honoring those lives well-lived, commemorating those worth remembering, who by their passing left their mark on the hearts of those who loved them.

The cemetery was behind us now. I turned down the street to my left, hanging a right and then another left, parking outside an old white house with a rusty iron gate.

"We're here."

The house was empty. The planters were dry and barren. Brown leaves hung onto dead stumps. The house itself was fine. It survived Maria, though you saw from the front where the branch of a neighboring tree knocked loose a few terracotta shingles. Dead leaves covered the driveway and an iron chain, complete with padlock, held the driveway gate in place to bar intruders. From the window you saw some furniture, but I knew most of it was gone. The walls were bare and the kitchen, always so vibrant and full of sights and smells, was empty. No one had lived there in years.

After Abu died, Irma moved back to NY with her daughters. At first, she rented the house to a friend, a couple from the church on the verge of financial ruin who needed a place to stay. When they moved, she asked her neighbor, Carlo, to look after the property. Carlo was old, a little younger than Abu, and my mother and I wondered if he could keep up with the work required to keep the house intact. She assured us he could. We weren't convinced. We tried to convince her to sell it, but she wouldn't budge, and after a while, my mother gave up bringing it up and Irma stopped talking to us all together. Abu was the one holding us all together, and without him, well, we lost the one thing keeping us together. When Janiece and I got married, she didn't come to the wedding.

I turned off the ignition and got out of the car. Carlo's house was bright blue with full planters to match. He' always had a bit of a green thumb, something he and Abu shared. He and Abu used to compete over their gardens, arguing about whose flowers were better and whose gardens grew the best mangos. Abu told me that Carlo cheated, that he brought plants in from the Home Depot in Ponce. Carlo denied it, though one time Abu made me look through his trash for evidence. Our search was inconclusive.

I hesitated at the door. The last time I saw Carlo was at Abu's funeral. I wondered if he remembered me, or would he be as confused to see me as I was nervous to see him? I debated going back to the car, but before I could talk myself out of ringing his bell, I rang the doorbell and waited.

The door opened slowly. A set of gray eyes peered from between the door and the doorway like a twin set of moons.

"Quien es?" The voice shivered and croaked out the words as if under an immense strain, like every syllable took work. It was Carlo, all right. I remembered his voice from my childhood. It used to scare me. The last time I saw him, he was still a pack-a-day smoker. Abu always used to chide him, saying he'd kill himself in the end. I wondered if he'd given up the habit.

In the best Spanish I could muster, I tried to explain who I was. The door widened and Carlo peeked his head out from behind the door chain.

His skin was pulled tight across his face. A thin line of gray hair hovered above his lips. He was bald now. What remained of his hair was cut tight and short above his ears like a laurel crown. He looked me up and down, weighing the man before him against the boy he remembered. His eyes lit up and he stepped out into the light.

"Jose's grandson, here, at my door, I can't believe it. How have you been?"

His English was choppy, but I understood him. I beckoned for Janiece to join me and introduced her to Carlo. He grabbed her hand and kissed it.

"She's beautiful, no?" He said with a wink, smiling at me like he was the first one to acknowledge her beauty. I agreed with him, and when he took her hand and led her inside, I couldn't help but laugh. Age had done very little to curtail his charm. I followed them through a narrow hallway covered in photographs in wooden frames. I noticed Abu in a few of them. It was easy to forget that he had a life outside of his family. I knew he did, but to see the evidence on the walls of Carlo's house was a reminder that there was still so much I didn't know about my grandfather.

We sat down in Carlo's kitchen in bright plastic chairs that squirmed whenever you moved. While we sat, Carlo got a pot of coffee going and rummaged about in the fridge before setting down a plate of cheese and crackers. He poured the coffee into a set of cracked mugs. The coffee was light and sweet and strong. I took a long, deep sip, scalding my tongue, but I didn't care. There was something nostalgic about his kitchen. It reminded me of Abu's kitchen: Irma, always busy by the stove, while Abu and I played dominoes and drank coffee. He'd never let me win. Even when I'd cry, he'd tell me to play again. What I didn't know was that he was teaching me, teaching me that failures could be lessons if we let them, and that perseverance was a necessary virtue. I heard the dominoes moving on the table, clacking together as he shuffled them, his laughter bouncing off the walls. If I closed my eyes, I almost saw him. His smile. The way he lit up a room. But he wasn't there, and all I had left were memories, memories and regrets, pale images obscured by a wall of fog.

Carlo got up from the table and returned with a ring of keys.

"I try my best to keep it clean," he said. "But it's in good shape. I figured you'd want to take a look around before you leave."

I nodded and thanked him, taking the keys from his hand and putting them in my pocket. I told him we'd be back in a few minutes, but he told us to take our time.

Part of me felt silly. It was an empty house and nothing else. But then again, maybe I was underestimating the power of place, and the ability of our senses to bring us back to those places our minds didn't dare go. I stood in front of the gate and twisted the key in the lock holding the chain in place.

It fell to the floor with a thud.

The chain lay on the floor like an iron snake bathing in the sun.

I stepped over the sleeping beast and forced the gate open. The motorized gate had fallen into disrepair, and after pushing the it open, I wondered how Carlo got into the house to clean.

The porch was empty. The hammocks lay limp on the floor, hanging from one side of the wall but not the other. I ran my hands along the fabric, feeling each stitch, trying to remember what it was like to sway back and forth in the early afternoon heat, a Coke in one hand and a pressed sandwich in another: free the way children are when everything was good, and life had yet to rear its ugly head.

We turned the corner. The garden was empty. The trees were torn down. All that was left was a square patch of dirt baking in the sun. It seemed so much bigger when I was a kid, but now that it was stripped bare, it seemed tragically small.

We walked back towards the front of the house and opened the front door. The house was empty. A few of Irma's precious mariposas hung from the walls but the pictures and furniture were gone. The rest of the house was pretty much the same. The bedrooms were empty, and only a few bedframes remained. Even Abu's office, which as a young boy seemed eternal, was blank. I left as quickly as I could, almost dragging Janiece behind me. I tied the chain around the fence and locked it in place.

Coming back here was a bad idea.

The car was quiet as we left Yauco. Janiece knew me enough to know that I needed my space. She sat with her head resting against the window, staring off into space, waiting for me to break the ice and speak. I was too lost in thought to think of something to say. I thought about driving us to his grave, but I knew there I'd find more of the same—the same empty feeling that filled me from stem to stern, the absence of emotion that's only brought on by regret, the apathy that fills you when you realize there's no going back, there's no fixing the past. There was only the reality of your choices and the consequences that followed in their wake. What I wanted was absolution, but if there was any left for me, I knew it wouldn't be found in front of his grave. We kept driving.

We pulled over a few miles out of town to eat lunch at a little stand serving empanadas and soda. The place looked familiar. Like a ship emerging from the fog, I remembered that Abu's river wasn't too far. I got up, stuffing the rest of my empanada into my mouth, and pulled out my phone. I didn't remember exactly how to get there, but I knew we were close. I looked at the map, zooming in and out trying to locate the river, a thin blue line in a field of green. It was only a few minutes away. I grabbed Janiece's hand and dragged her back to the car.

She asked where we were going. I smiled and told her it was a surprise. With one hand on the wheel and the other holding my phone, we navigated through the town until we hit a dirt road. I slowed down, inching along, looking down every few seconds to make sure we went in the right direction.

We were close. I pulled the car onto the side of the road and got out. Beside us, the foliage extended over our heads. A great wall of green between us and the river's edge. I pushed aside the brush and opened a way for us through the trees. A small dirt path emerged, sloping gently downward as it wound its way through the overgrowth. I remembered walking this path before, Abu in front of me, no longer leaning on his cane, but like a panther moving lithely through the wood, light on his feet, like his youth returned the further downhill we went.

I saw it through the tree line, a clear line of water gently moving through the hillside, curving around rocks, forming little pools where the water slowed and deepened. I took off my shoes and put my feet in the running water. Janiece did the same and sat beside me. We were alone. All we heard was our breathing, the river, and the wind moving through the trees.

"Abu used to bring me here when I was a kid," I said. "I think I was six when we came here for the first time. I was scared, barely knew how to swim. The water seemed deeper then. The river, wilder. I stood on the shore for what seemed like ages while Abu watched me. He didn't say anything at first. He wanted me to face my fear, but he didn't chide me for it, he just waited, waiting for the right moment to come alongside me. I turned around and pouted on the shore, afraid of the water and upset at myself. Abu got up from where he sat and sat beside me. We sat there for some time, and then he took me by the hand and led me to the edge of the river. He waded into the water and waited for me to join him. He was old. He probably strained his back. But he wasn't selfish. He knew that this moment wasn't for him, it was for me."

"You never told me that story," Janiece replied.

"Yeah, maybe I wasn't ready to share it."

"What made you ready now?"

"I don't know. Maybe it's being back here, facing it after all these years, the guilt, I mean. I failed him in the end. I was young and selfish and scared. I never said goodbye and it ate away at me for years. Part of me blocked those stories out because I thought I didn't deserve their comfort. But being back here, I'm ready to remember. I'm tired of running."

Before my wife could reply, I slipped off the bank and into the water and ducked my head under the current.

The whole world went silent.

There, under the gentle tug of the water, I let myself drift, for the first time allowing myself to remember. The pain was still there, but for once it felt good, as if the sudden stab of memory was a reminder that I was, indeed, alive.

When I emerged from the surface, I felt lighter, and for a moment the sky was bluer, and the water cooler, as if the whole world had changed in an instant, but when I looked over at Janiece, I knew what it was that was changed. It dawned on me that my grandfather never asked me to be anything other than me, and if he could accept all of me, the good times and the pain, then maybe to honor him meant remembering it all. I smiled and pulled Janiece in with me, and as we lay lazy in the river, I swore I saw Abu cooling his feet on the bank smiling back at me.

www.ingramcontent.com/pod-product-compliance
Lightning Source LLC
Chambersburg PA
CBHW062112080426
42734CB00012B/2837